H.I.S.WORD
BIBLICAL HEBREW
(101)

אֶת

COLOR EDITION
By JediYAH Melek

Table of Contents

Table of Contents

Did YASHUA use Biblical Hebrew?:

The **Dead Sea Scrolls** are the oldest Hebrew scriptures that have been discovered on earth. They date back to as early as 356 B.C. This means that there is archaelogical evidence proving that Israelites used Biblical Hebrew more than 300 years before YASHUA was born.

The Dead Sea Scrolls

After the Babylonian captivity of Israel, Hebrew scribes such as Daniel, Ezra, Nehemiah, The Maccabees, YASHUA and the Holy Apostles etc. wrote scripture using Biblical Hebrew instead of Paleo Hebrew. The spoken language and grammar rules remained the same, only the style of lettering changed. The Dead Sea Scrolls prove the style of Hebrew used after the return from exile.

יהוה

Yod (jot)

Matthew 5:17 **Think not that I am come to destroy the Torah (Law), or the prophets: I am not come to destroy, but to fulfil.**
Matthew 5:18 **For verily I say unto you, Till heaven and earth pass, one** *jot (Yod)* **or one** *tittle (Qotz)* **shall in no wise pass from the Torah, till all be fulfilled.**

Matthew 5:18 כִּי אָמֵן אֹמֵר אֲנִי לָכֶם עַד כִּי־יַעַבְרוּ
הַשָּׁמַיִם וְהָאָרֶץ לֹא תַעֲבֹר *יוֹד* אַחַת אוֹ־*קוֹץ* אֶחָד מִן־הַתּוֹרָה
עַד אֲשֶׁר יְקֻיַּם הַכֹּל:

• Qotz
(Tittle)

• Yod
(Jot)

Biblical Hebrew

In **Matthew 5:18** YASHUA makes a reference to the Hebrew letter *Yod*. *Yod* is the smallest letter in Biblical Hebrew. In Paleo Hebrew *Yod* is the same height as all the other letters. **Qotz (or tittle)** is the curved tip at the top of the letter *Yod* **that only appears in Biblical Hebrew,** not Paleo Hebrew.

Yod (jot)

Paleo Hebrew Yod does not have a Qotz (tittle).

Paleo Hebrew

From the direct words of YASHUA in Matthew 5:18 as well as from the ancient Dead Sea Scrolls we can definitively know that **Biblical Hebrew was used by the Messiah, the Apostles and many of the Prophets.**

Matthew 5:17 **Think not that I am come to destroy the Torah (Law), or the prophets: I am not come to destroy, but to fulfil.**

So if YASHUA did not come to destroy Torah, but to fulfil it, then the Biblical Hebrew He used is part of that fulfilment.

We must study to show ourselves approved in order to properly discern the truth concerning our Hebrew language and culture.

2 Timothy 2:15 **Study to shew thyself approved unto ELOHIM, a workman that needeth not to be ashamed, rightly dividing the word of truth.**

Are you ready?

Lets begin!!!

· Aleph
· Sound: **Silent**

Aleph = Head

Aleph is the 1st letter of the Hebrew Aleph-bet. It is a **silent letter** that only takes on the sound of an associated vowel symbol.

The Hebrew language is written from right-to-left.

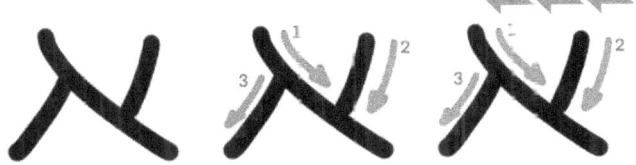

Hebrew Vowels or *Niqqudim:*
Hebrew **vowels** are a series of dots or dashes that are placed below or above Hebrew **consonants**.

We'll start by learning the first two symbols:

Qamatz & Patakh

Aa as in Aardvark   A as in About

Hebrew Vowels:

The Hebrew vowels *qamatz* and *patakh* sound nearly identical but the *patakh* has a slightly shorter sound than the *qamatz*.

Let's practice writing our first two vowels!

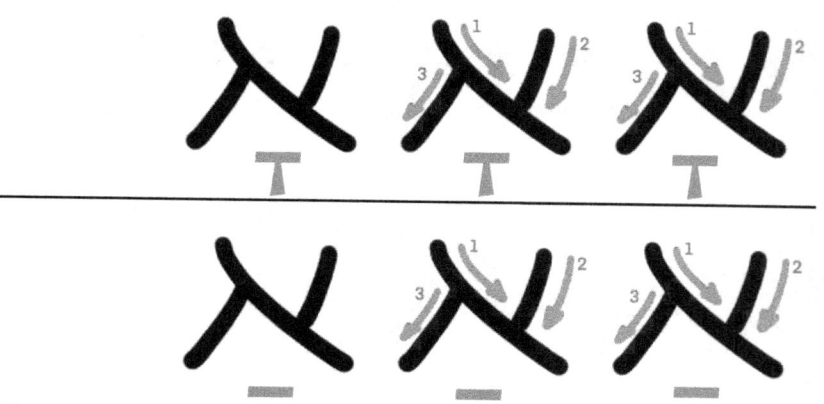

When reading Hebrew letters, **the consonant is always pronounced first and the vowel after**. *Qamatz* and *Patakh* are always placed underneath its corresponding letter.

The Difference Between Vowels and Consonants:

In english, vowels are considered to be the letters a-e-i-o-u and sometimes 'y'. The real difference between vowels and consonants is:

1. Vowels are sounds that cause **the throat to vibrate** when vocalized.
2. Consonant letters are **pronounced from the lips** and do not vibrate the throat.

Test The Spirit

We can actually feel the difference between pronouncing vowels and consonants. Place your hand over your throat and say: a-e-i-o-u. Did you feel your throat vibrate? Now pronouced consonant letters like b-c-d-f-g etc. All of these sounds are made from the lips and not from the throat. It is impossible to have any language without the use of both vowels and consonants.

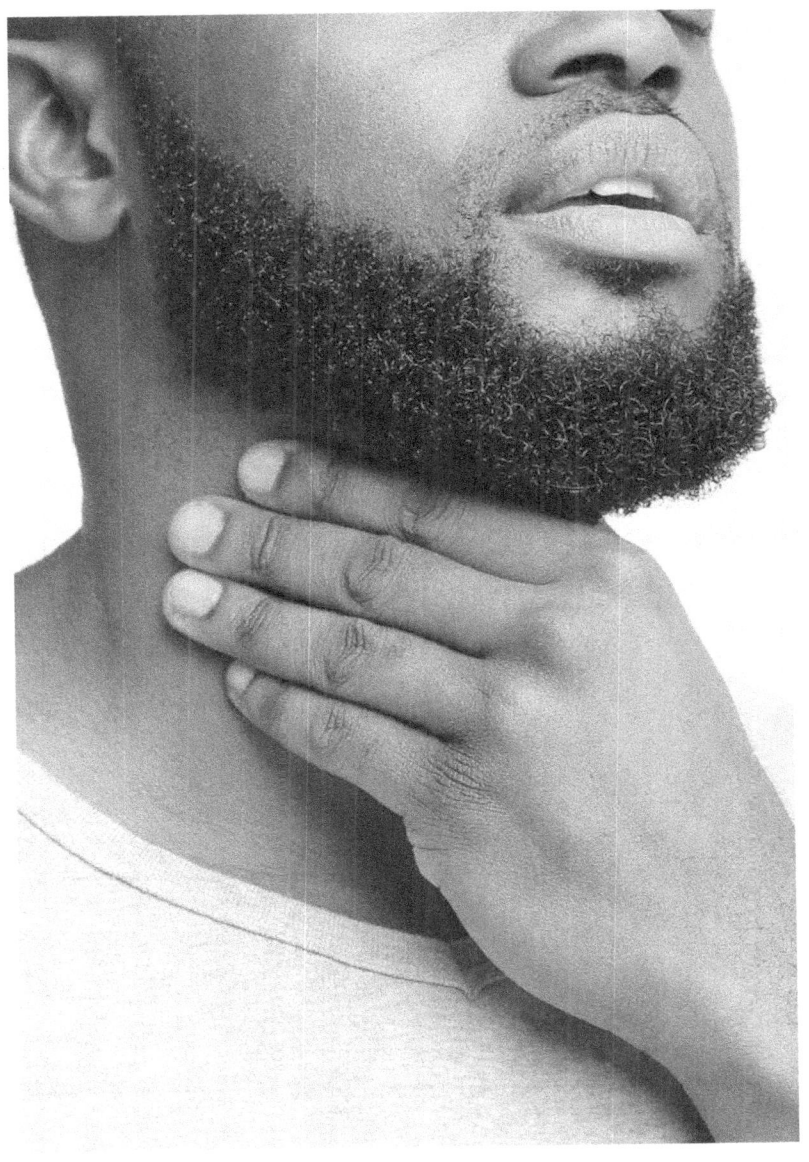

Qamatz
Long Vowel:
Aah

Patakh
Short Vowel:
Ah

• *Bet*
• Sound: **b/v**

Bet = House

Bet is the 2nd letter of the Hebrew Aleph-bet. **When *Bet* has a dot in its center, it is pronounced as a 'b' as in ball.**

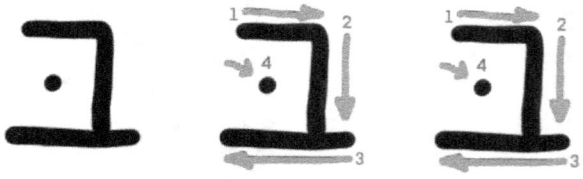

When *Bet* does not have a dot in its center, it is sometimes pronounced 'v' as in vine.

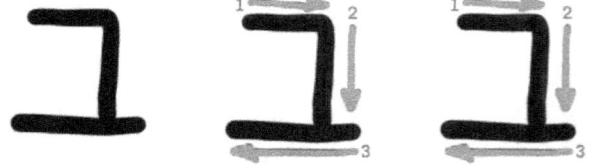

Fun Fact:
The english word 'alphabet' comes from the first 2 Hebrew letters: ***Aleph-Bet***.

Ready to Read

Now you are ready to starting reading. *Remember that when a vowel is written under a consonant, the consonant is pronounced first then the vowel.* **When an Aleph is missing a vowel then Aleph becomes a silent letter**.

$$\text{(silent)} = א$$

$$אַ = אַ + א$$

$$בָּ = אַ + בָּ$$

Reading Practice

Remember to read Hebrew from right-to-left.

בָּא	אַב	בְ	בַּ	בְ	בּ	א	אָ
ba	ab	va	ba	v	b	(silent)	a

בָּאב	בָּאב	בַּב	בָּב
bab	bav	bav	bab

Always Remember

Aleph is a silent letter. It will only have a sound if a vowel is attached to it.

Hebrew Vocabulary

The First Hebrew Word
The first word in Hebrew is made by simply putting the first two letters together.

$$\text{אָב} = \text{ב} + \text{אָ}$$

AB is the first Hebrew word and it means 'Father.'
Each individual Hebrew letter also has its own meaning.

Aleph = Head

Bet = House

Aleph + Bet = Head (of the) House

or

Father

Head	**House**	**Father**
	+ 	= 

Hebrew Vocabulary			
Father (Ab) =		**Coming (Ba) =**	

Write each Hebrew word 3 times:

Father (Ab)   _____   אָב

_____   אָב

_____   אָב

Coming (Ba)   _____   בָּא

_____   בָּא

_____   בָּא

Father (*is) coming! =		אָב בָּא!

*In Hebrew the word 'is' does not exist. It is already an understood concept that is not written.

· *Gimel*
· Sound: **g**

Gimel = Camel

Gimel is the 3rd letter of the Hebrew Aleph-bet. **It is pronounced 'g' as in good.**

ג גֿ גֿ

Reading Practice:
When *Gimel* is at the beginning of a word it will have a dot (*dagesh*) in the center of it. However, the sound does not change.

בָּאֵג	גַ	אָב	א	בַּג	גַב	גַ	ג
bag	ga	ab	(silent)	bag	gav	ga	g

אָבַג	בָּאֵב	בַּ	בַּגַב	גַג
abag	ba'av	ba	bagav	gag

Matching Sets:

Let's see how well you know your stuff. Match each Hebrew item with the correct English word.

Aleph   גּ

Patakh   בָּא

Gimel   אָב

Qamatz   בּ

Bet   ָ

Father   ב

Coming   ַ

Vet   א

ד

 **Dalet**

• Sound: **d**

Dalet = Door

Dalet is the 4th letter of the Hebrew Aleph-bet. **It is pronounced 'd' as in door. When Dalet is at the beginning of a word it has a dot (dagesh) in it.**

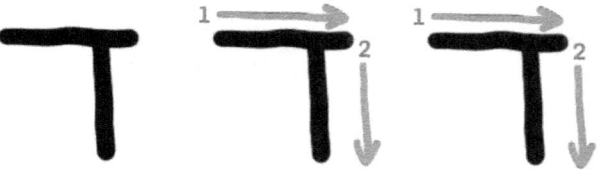

Roof = גּג

(Gag)

Fish = דּג

(Dag)

Troop = גּד

(Gad)

Lost =
אָבַד (Avad)

Write (*Kitov*):
Write each new Hebrew word across the line from right-to-left.

דָּג

_____

גָּד

_____

אָבַד

_____

Translate (*Targem*):
Can you translate each English word?

Fish = _____

Lost = _____

Troop = _____

Roof = _____

Coming = _____

·Heh
· Sound: h

Heh = Behold/Window

Heh is the 5th letter of the Hebrew Aleph-bet. **It is pronounced 'h' as in house. When *Heh* is at the end of a word it is silent.**

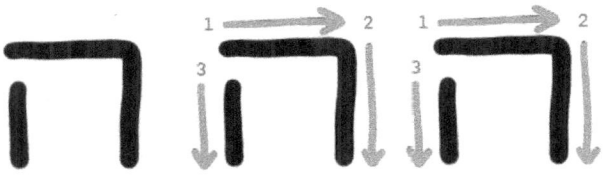

When a Heh is attached to the beginning of a word, it is translated as "the". Here's an example:

The Fish = הַדָּג = דָּג + הַ   Fish = דָּג
(Ha'Dag)

The Father = הָאָב = אָב + הָ   Father = אָב
(Ha'Ab)

Meditate = הָגָה   Offering = הַבְהָב
(Hagah)   (Havhav)

Meditated = הָגָה (Masculine)

Suppport Hebrew Music. Download **Yahudah Shalom's** album *"Manna From Heaven"* today!

Write (*Kitov*):
Write the Hebrew words for each picture below:

The **Father**

_____ =

The **Fish**

_____ =

The **Roof**

_____ =

The **Troop**

_____ =

Loved = אָהַב (Masculine)
(Ahav)

Loved = אָהֲבָה (Feminine)
(Ahavah)

Translate (*Targem*):
Can you translate each phrase into English?

1. הָדָג בָּא הַגָּג.

_____

2. הָאָב אָהַב הָדָג.

_____

3. הַגָּד אָבַד הַדָג.

_____

E-class Vowels:

Hebrew **vowels** are a series of dots or dashes that are placed below or above Hebrew **consonants**.

The next vowel (*niqqud*) makes an e-sound:

Segol

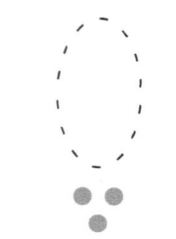

e as in bet

Read Aloud (*Haq'rey*):
Let's practice reading with *segol*. **Segol is a vowel with 3 dots underneath a Hebrew letter.** It is pronounced like an '**e**' in **bet**.

הֶ דֶ גֶ בֶ אֶ
(heh) (deh) (geh) (veh) (beh) (eh)

אֶג אֶד בֶג הֶד דֶד בֶד
(Eg) (Ed) (Beg) (Hed) (Ded) (bed)

הֶבֶב גֶדֶב הֶאֶד בֶגֶד אֶבֶד
(Hevev) (Gedev) (Hed) (Beged) (Eved)

Egg

_____

Beg

_____

Dead

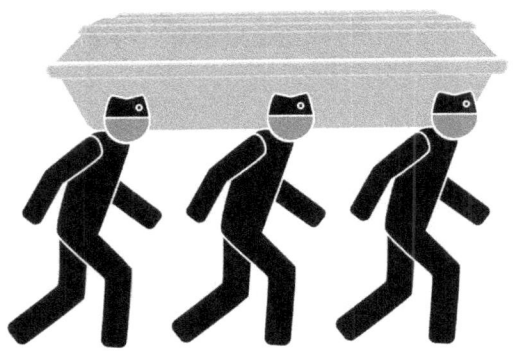

_____

Bed

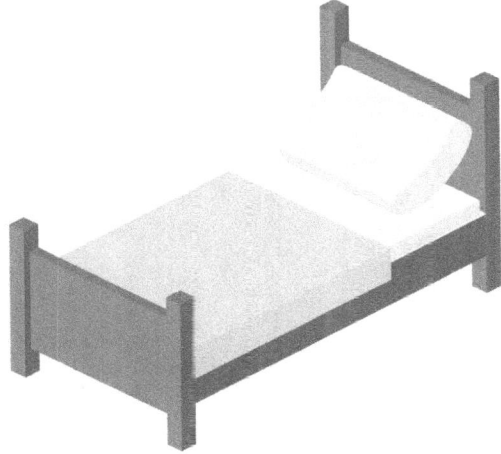

_____

Clothes = בֶּגֶד
(Beged)

ר

• *Waw*

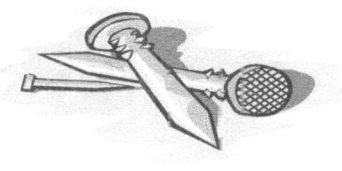

Waw = Nail/Hook

• Sound: **w/o**

Waw is the 6th letter of the Hebrew Aleph-bet. **It is pronounced 'w' as in wall.**

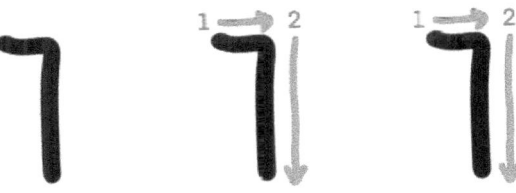

Write (*Kitov*):
Use Hebrew letters to write each english word:

Web

Wed

Hook = וָו

O-class Vowels:
When *Waw* has a dot (*Holem*) above it, it is pronounced like an 'o' as in **o**pen.

וֹ וֹ וֹ

Reading Practice:
Read each Hebrew item below. The english transliteration is under each one.

דּוֹדָה דּוֹד וֹו דּוֹ אוֹ הוֹ בּוֹ גּוֹ
Dodah   Dod   Wo   Do   Oh   Ho   Bo   Go

הוֹבוֹ הוֹדָה גּוֹא הוֹדָה הוֹד בּוֹא
Hobo   Go   Hodah   Hod   Bo

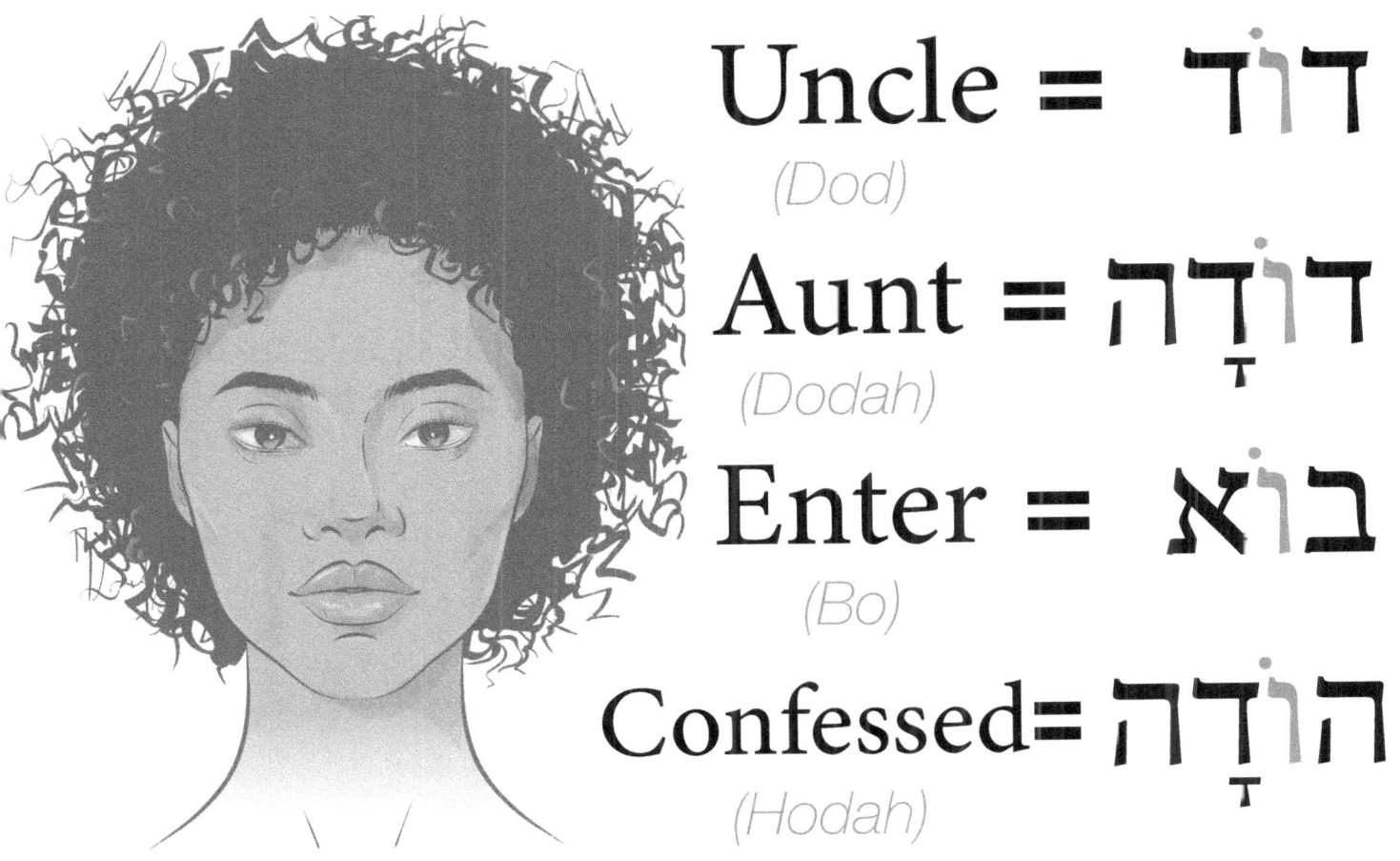

Uncle = דּוֹד
(Dod)

Aunt = דּוֹדָה
(Dodah)

Enter = בוֹא
(Bo)

Confessed = הוֹדָה
(Hodah)

Beauty = הוֹד (Hod)

So far we have learned that the letter וֹ (**waw**) has 2 different sounds:

1. Waw וֹ = 'w' as in wall

2. Waw with a dot above it וֹ = 'o' as in open

Now we will learn the 3rd sound of the letter ו (*waw*):

U-class **Vowels:**

When *Waw* has a dot (*Shureq*) inside of it, it is pronounced like an 'u' as in uber or 'oo' as in true.

Read Aloud *(Haq'rey)*:
Let's practice reading with *Shureq*. *Shureq* is a vowel with a dot inside of the letter *Waw*. It is pronounced 'u' as in uber or 'oo' as in true.

הוּ דוּ גוּ בוּ בֻּ אוּ
Hu   Doo Goo Vu Boo Oo

בוּא גוּא הוּא בוּד דוּד גוּד
Boo Goo Hu Bood Dood Good

Overcame = גּוּד

He = הוּא

Pot = דּוּד

Vowel Abbreviations:

You have already learned that the letter *Waw* can be used to pronounce O-class vowels וֹ (*Holem*) and U-class vowels וּ (*Shureq*). Sometimes a וֹ (*Holem*) and a וּ (*Shureq*) can be abbreviated with the following symbols:

O-class **Vowels:** וֹ = ◌ֹ

U-class **Vowels:** וּ = ◌ֻ

The pronunciation of each of the vowels remains the same when they are abbreviated.

O-class **Vowels:**

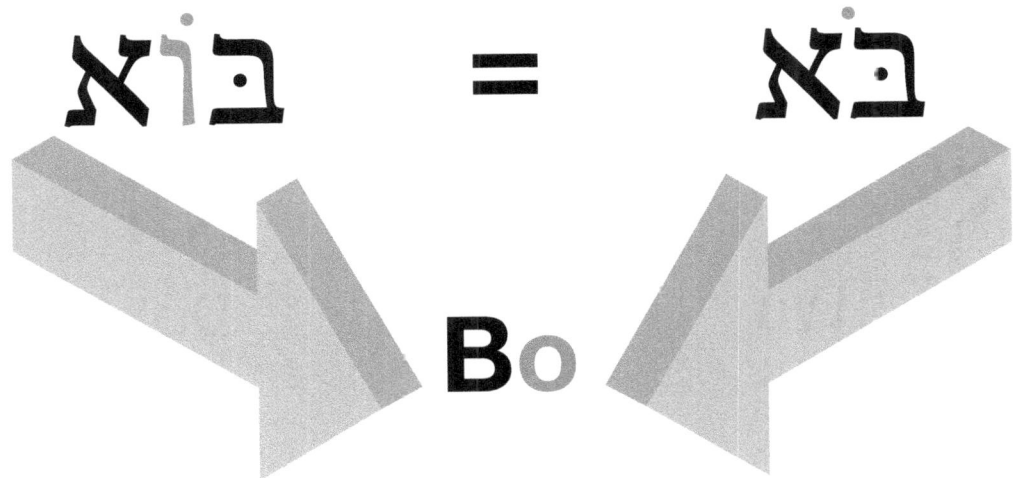

בּוֹא = בֹּא

Bo

U-class **Vowels:**

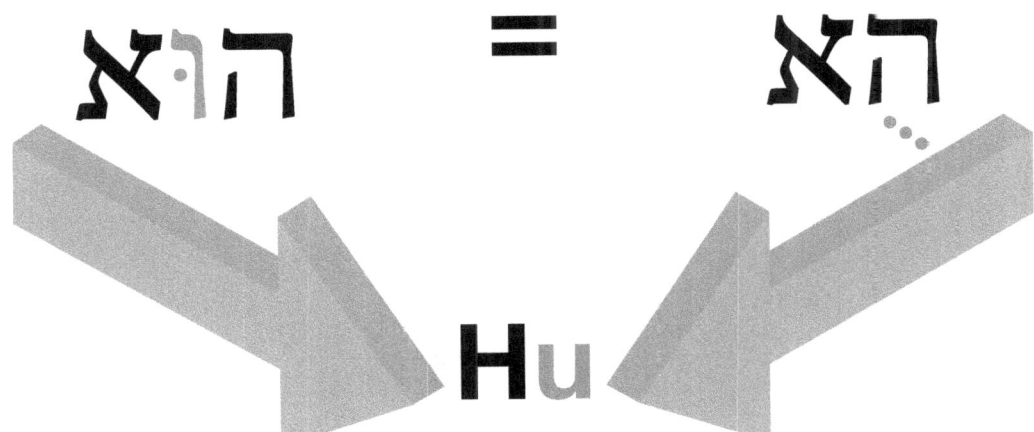

הוּא = הֻא

Hu

Read Aloud *(Haq'rey)*:
Now let's practice reading with **O** and **U** class vowels.

גָא	גוֹ	בָּא	בוֹ	בָּא	בוֹ
Gu	Gu	Bo	Bo	Bu	Bu

וָא	וּ	הָא	הוּ	דָּא	דוֹ
Wo	Wu	Ho	Hu	Do	Do

Holem =

Qibbutz =

Matching Sets:

Let's see how well you know your stuff. Match each Hebrew item with the correct English word.

Holem (Oh)

Shureq (U/Oo)

Patakh (Ah)

Qamatz (Aah)

Holem-Waw (Oh)

Qibbutz (U/Oo)

Segol (Eh)

Waw

ז

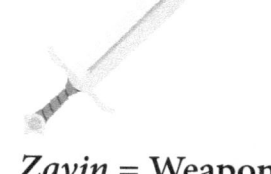

• *Zayin*
• Sound: **z**

Zayin = Weapon

Zayin is the 7th letter of the Hebrew Aleph-bet. **It is pronounced 'z' as in zebra.**

Gold = זָהָב
(Zahav)

This = זֶה
(Zeh)

Overflow =
(Zuv)

זוּב

Dowry = זֶבֶד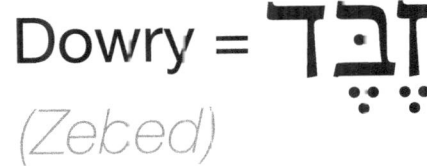
(Zebed)

Translate (*Targem*):
Can you translate each phrase into English?

1. הוּא אָהַב הַזָהָב.

---

2. הָדוֹדָה אָהֲבָה הַזֶבֶד.

3. זֶה גָּד גּוּד.

_____

4. הָאָב הָגָה.

_____

5. הָאָב הוּא אָהַב הַבֶּגֶד.

_____

Hebrew Crosswords

Fill in the crossword puzzle in Hebrew by using clues from the english words below.

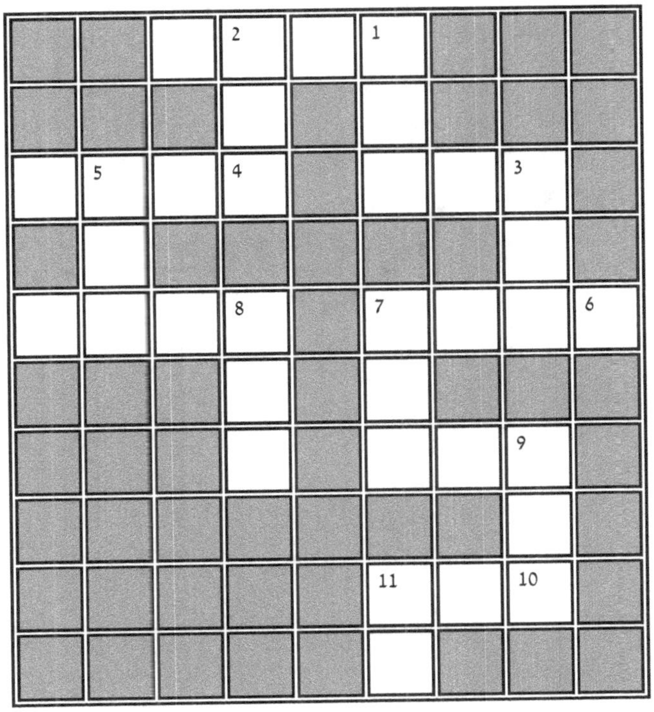

Across

1 Loved (f)

3 Dowry

4 Aunt

6 Offering

8 Confessed

9 He

10 Pot

Down

1 Lost

2 Clothes

3 Overflow

5 Uncle

7 Enter

8 Meditate

9 Beauty

11 Fish

Congratulations!!!

You are now reading, writing and translating Biblical Hebrew!

⋅ *Khet*
⋅ Sound: **kh**

Khet = Fence

Khet is the 8th letter of the Hebrew Aleph-bet. *Khet* has a unique sound that is rarely used in english. **It is pronounced the 'kh' in Khanukah.**

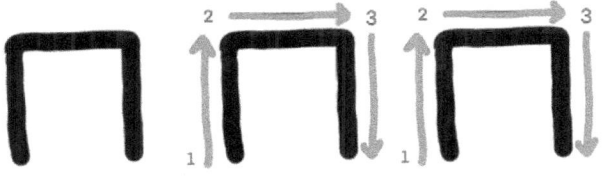

seer = חֹזֶה

Feast = חַג

Brother =

אָח

(Akh)

One = אֶחָד

(Ekhad)

Circle = חוּג

(Khug)

Locust =

חָגָב

When A Word Ends With A

We have learned that in Hebrew the consonant is pronounced before the vowel. However, there is an exception when a word *ends* with a *Khet* and a *patakh*.

Bage'AKH instead of Bagekha   בָּגֶךְ

Deve'AKH instead of Devekha   דְּבֶךְ

Aze'AKH instead of Azekha   אָזֶךְ

Hu'AKH instead of Hukha   הוּחַ

Khet and **Heh** look very similar. Can you tell the difference between them? Circle each **Khet** below and put a square around each **Heh**.

ב	ל	ס	ו	ט	ח	א
נ	פ	ח	כ	ח	ע	ר
ו	מ	שׁ	צ	י	ס	ח
ח	ר	שׁ	ז	ה	שׁ	נ
ץ	ז	כ	ח	ב	ה	ק
ה	צ	ק	ה	ח	ף	ה
ח	ה	ג	מ	ל	ת	ו

How many **Khets** do you see? _____   How many **Hehs** do you see? _____

Use the number of Khets to find the chapter and the number of Hehs to find this verse:

Proverbs ___:___ Hear; for I will speak of excellent things; and the opening of my lips shall be right things.

• Tet

• Sound: t

Tet = Basket

Tet is the 9th letter of the Hebrew Aleph-bet. **It is pronounced 't' as in tall.**

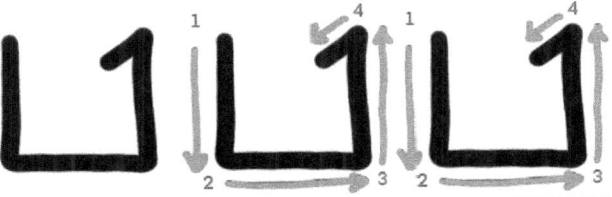

Good = טוֹב

(Tov)

Spin = טָוָה

Sin = חָטָא
(Khata)

Archer = טָחָה

Translate (*Targem*):
Can you translate each phrase into Hebrew?

When writing a sentence in Hebrew the *noun (person, place or thing)* is placed before the **adjective (a word that describes a noun)**. In the example below, *brother is the noun* and **good is the adjective**. When translating into Hebrew the *noun* comes before the **adjective**.

1. He is a good brother.

הוּא אָח טוֹב

*Remember that in Hebrew there is no word for '*is*' or '*a*.'

2. The archer is good.

_____

3. The aunt loved the uncle.

_____

4. The brother is a Seer.

_____

5. This pot is gold.

_____

ל

Yod = Hand

• *Yod*
• Sound: **y**

Yod is the 10th letter of the Hebrew Aleph-bet. **It is pronounced 'y' as in yes. Yod is the smallest letter in Hebrew. It floats above the guideline.**

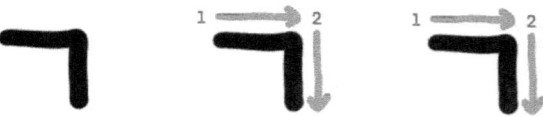

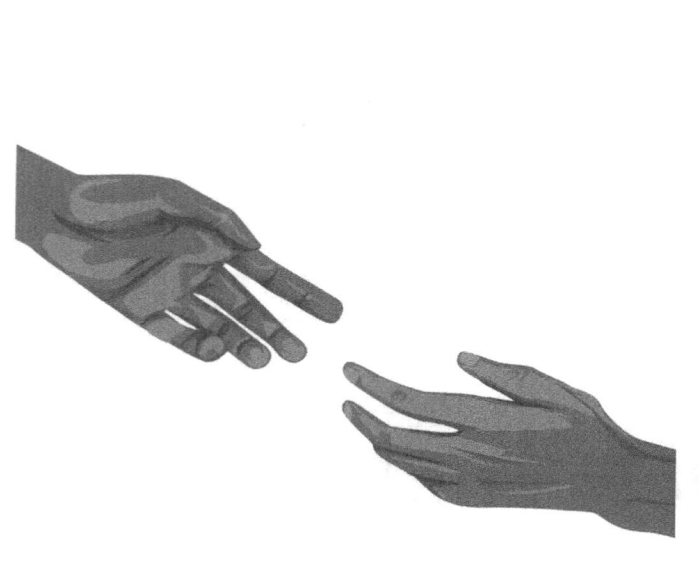

Hand = יָד   (be) Successful = יָטַב

When The Past, The Present and The Future Are ONE...
When The Eternal Nature of The Most High (Past, Present and Future) are united we have:

YA-HO-WAH

HE WAS-HE IS-HE WILL BE

Or

"The Eternal One"

Revelation 1:8

"I am Aleph and Taw, saith *YAHOWAH*, WHICH IS, AND WHICH WAS AND WHICH IS TO COME, the Almighty."

1. ‏יַהְוֶה הוּא טוֹב.‏

---

2. ‏יַהְוֶה הוּא אֶחָד.‏

---

3. ‏יַהְוֶה גוּד חָטָא.‏

4. הַיָד־יַהוָֹה בָּא.

---

5. יַהוָֹה הוּא אָב טוֹב.

Together = יָחַד

(Yakhad)

I-class Vowels:.

The next vowel (*niqqud*) makes an i-sound:

Khireq

i as in it

Read Aloud *(Haq'rey)*:
Let's practice reading with *khireq*. ***Khireq* is a
vowel with 1 dot underneath a Hebrew letter.** It is
pronounced like an '**i**' in i**t**.

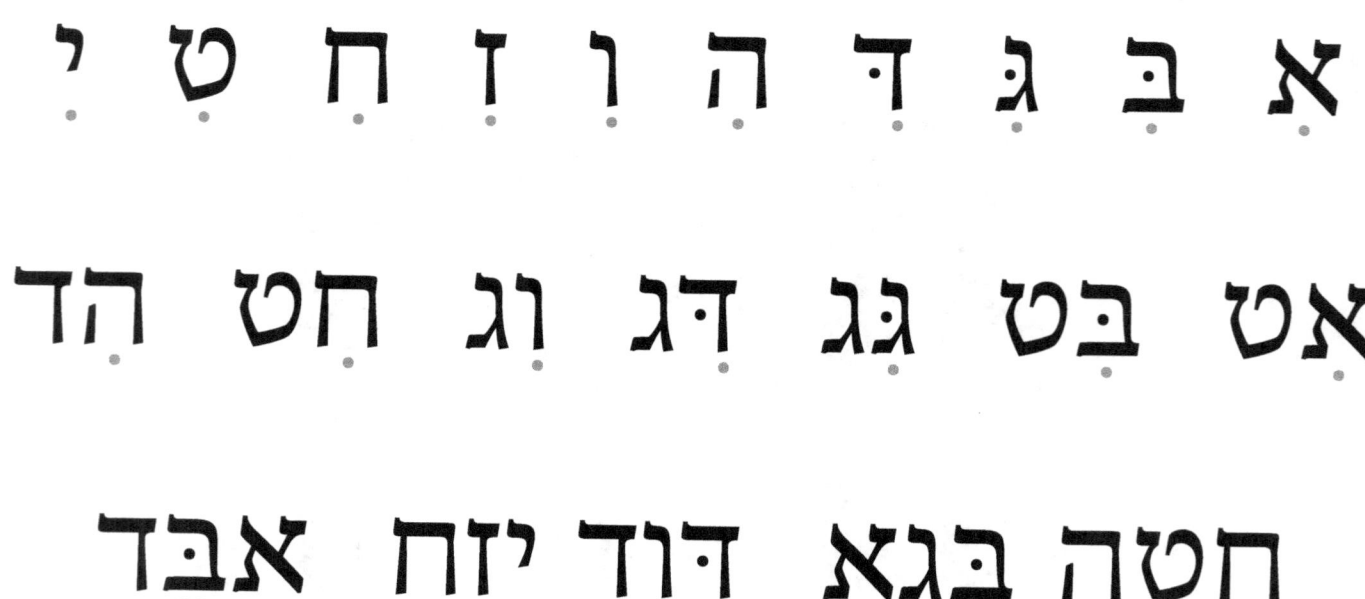

I-class **Vowels**:.

The next vowel (*niqqud*) makes an ee-sound:

Khireq-Yod

i as in mach**i**ne
ee as in s**ee**n

Whenever a *khireq* is immediately followed by a *yod*, the vowel changes from an *'i'* as in *it* to an *'i'* as in **mach*i*ne. This is called a *khireq-yod* vowel.**

Read Aloud *(Haq'rey)*:
Let's practice reading with *khireq-yod. Khireq-yod* is pronounced like an *'i'* in mach**i**ne or as an *'ee'* s**ee**n.

חִי זִי וִי הִי דִי גִי בִּי אִי

וִיט בִּיט הִיד וִיד בִּיד הִיט

יָחִיד יָחִידָה הֲבִיא הֱבִיאָה הֲבִיאָה

David = דָּוִד   Only = יָחִיד

My Father = אָבִי

(He) Was = הָיָה   My Brother = אָחִי

Translate (*Targem*):
Can you translate each phrase into Hebrew?

1. David was the only brother.

_____

2. David was successful.

_____

3. My father was a good archer.

_____

4. My brother lost the grasshopper.

_____

5. The Seer overcame the sin.

_____

6. The gold pot overflowed.

_____

•*Kaph*
• Sound: **k**

Kaph = Palm

Kaph is the 11th letter of the Hebrew Aleph-bet. **It is pronounced 'k' as in kick.**

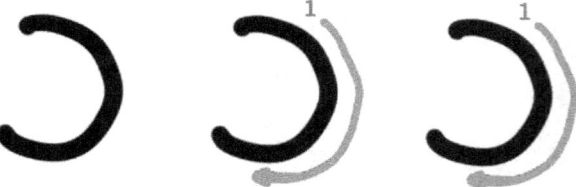

When *Kaph* is at the end of a word, a *Kaph-Sophit* is used. *Kaph-Sophit* has a different shape than a regular *Kaph* but the **sound is the same.**

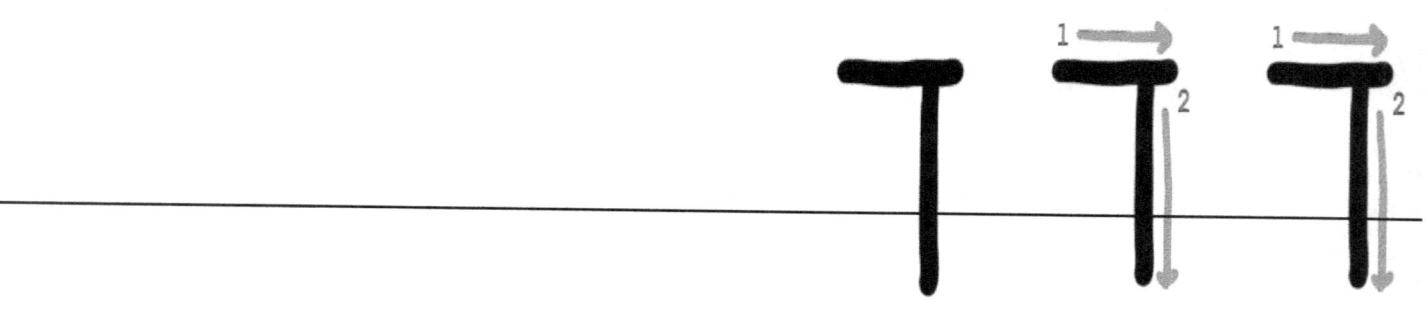

Kaph-Sophit looks like the letter Dalet, **but they extend below the guide-line.**

Reading Practice:

When *Kaph* is at the beginning of a word it will have a dot (*dagesh*) in the center of it. However, the sound does not change.

Star = כּוֹכָב

Heavy = כּוֹבֶד

Strength = כֹּחַ

(Koakh)

Pitcher = כַּד

Kaph-Sophit and **Dalet** look very similar. Can you tell the difference between them? Circle each **Kaph-Sophit** below and put a square around each **Dalet**.

ר	ל	ז	ך	ך	ח	ו
ך	ד	ב	כ	ח	ע	ך
ק	ך	שׁ	צ	ך	ל	ד
ח	ר	שׁ	נ	ה	שׁ	נ
ץ	ז	כ	ע	ך	ך	ע
ד	צ	ק	ך	ד	ף	ך
א	ה	ך	ג	ל	ת	ו

How many Dalets do you see? ___ How many Kaph-Sophits do you see? ___
Use the number of Dalets to find the chapter and the number of Kaph-Sophits to find this verse:

Sirach ___:___ Wisdom exalteth her children, and layeth hold of them that seek her.

ל

• **Lamed**

• Sound: l

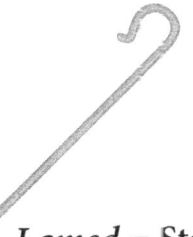

Lamed = Staff

Lamed is the 12th letter of the Hebrew Aleph-bet. **It is pronounced 'l' as in love.**

Capture = לָכַד

No = לֹא

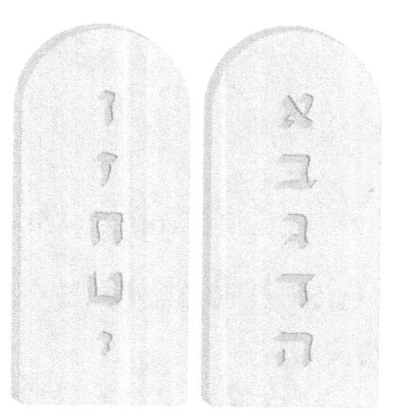

Tablet =

לוּחַ

(Luakh)

Alone =

לְבַד

Burn =

לָהַט

The *Sh'wa:*

The *Sh'wa* is not a vowel, **it is a symbol used to divide a word into syllables**. There are two (2) types of *Sh'wa's:*

1. *Sh'wa* **Na (The Moving *Sh'wa*)**

Sh'wa at the beginning of a word

The Moving *Sh'wa*:
When a *Sh'wa* is at the beginning of a word then only the sound of the letter is pronounced (without any vowel sound).

Read Aloud (*Haq'rey*):
Let's practice reading with *Sh'wa*. A *Sh'wa* at the beginning of a word means that only the sound of the letter is pronounced.

גְדוּלָה	גְדוּד	גְּאֻלָה	בְּלִי	בְּכִי
(G'dulah)	(G'dud)	(G'ulah)	(B'liy)	(E'kiy)

יְהוּדָה	גְּלִידָה	לְחִי	לְאֹט	לְבַד
(Y'hudah)	(G'liydan)	(L'khiy)	(L'ot)	(L vad)

2. Sh'wa **Nakh (The Resting Sh'wa)**

זָבְחָה

Sh'wa at the end of a syllable

The Resting Sh'wa:
When a Sh'wa is at the end of a syllable, or the end of a word it is always silent.

Read Aloud (Haq'rey):
Let's practice reading with Sh'wa. A **Sh'wa** at the end of a syllable is always silent.

אֵיךְ אָבְדוּ זָבְחָה חָטְאָה
(Khatah) (Zavkhah) (Avdu) (Eyk)

אָבִיךְ טָבְלָה יָלְדוּ אָחִיךְ
(Akhiyk) (Yaldu) (Tavlah) (Abiyk)

Sh'wa Pairs:

Sometimes *sh'wa* can be paired with another vowel (*qamatz, patakh* or *segol*). **These type of *sh'wa* pairs do not create new vowels, the *sh'wa* only shortens the sound of the other vowel.**

Qamatz + *Sh'wa* =
short *Aah* vowel   ָ   +   ְ   =   ָֽ

Patakh + *Sh'wa* =
short *Ah* vowel   ַ   +   ְ   =   ַֽ

Segol + *Sh'wa* =
short *E* vowel   ֶ   +   ְ   =   ֶֽ

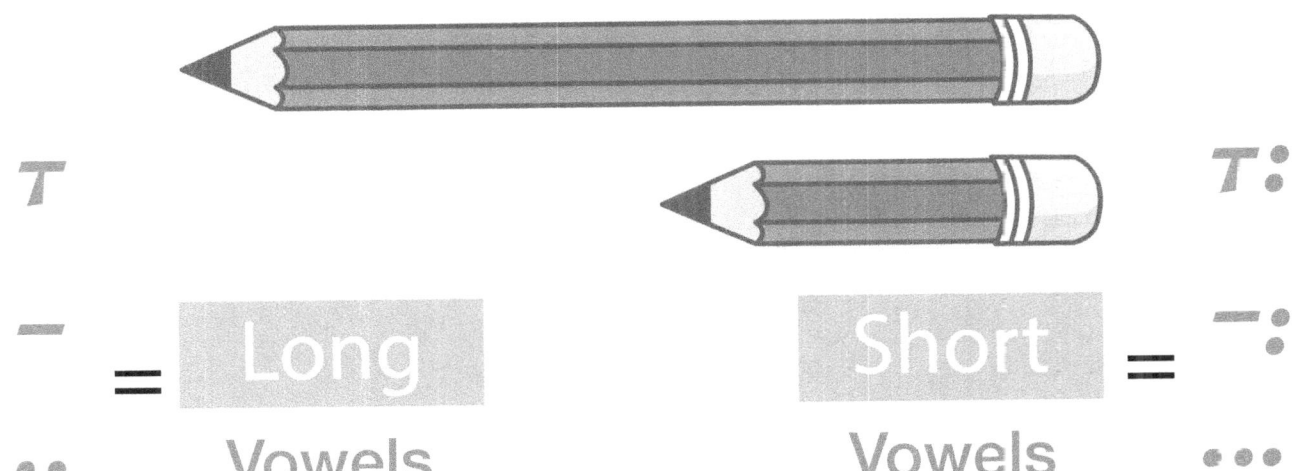

ָ

ָֽ

ָ   =   Long   Short   =   ַֽ

ְ   Vowels   Vowels   ֶֽ

 **• Mem**

• Sound: m

Mem = Water

Mem is the 13th letter of the Hebrew Aleph-bet. **It is pronounced 'm' as in mom.**

When ***Mem*** is at the end of a word, a ***Mem-Sophit*** is used. ***Mem-Sophit*** has a different shape than a regular ***Mem*** but the sound is the same.

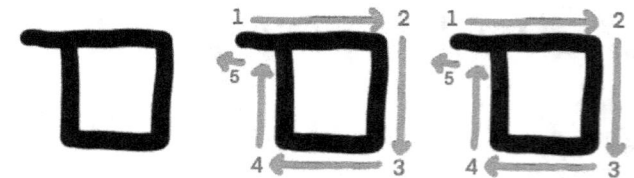

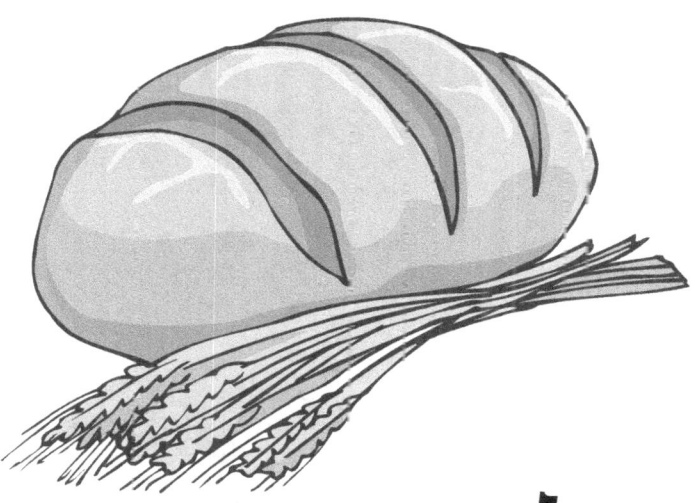

Fight = מִלְחָמָה

Bread = לֶחֶם

Angel = מַלְאָךְ

King = מֶלֶךְ

Tower = מִגְדָּל
(Migdal)

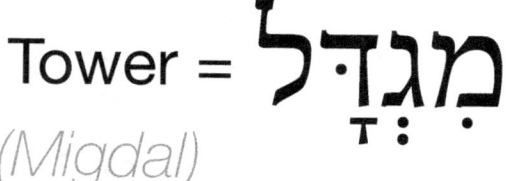

Water = מַיִם

66

Name: _____

Hebrew Word Search

Find the hidden english words by using clues from the Hebrew words below.

```
            D   T   F   H
        B   A   D   R   A   F   A   S
    G   E   I   Z   Y   Y   B   I   N   B
    R   V   D   V   L   B   N   C   R   D
B   A   O   A   E   U   D   I   O   T   R   F
D   O   E   G   R   V   R   T   E   A   T   Y
G   H   N   N   R   C   H   L   T   S   L   R
S   A   O   T   L   E   B   S   A   N   E   E
    P   G   E   R   A   E   E   O   H   N
    O   I   N   T   N   F   S   C   O   F
        O   N   I   E   O   R   L   J
            O   K   A   A
```

Hebrew Words Clues

1. חֹזֶה
2. חַג
3. אַח
4. אֶחָד
5. חוּג
6. טוֹב
7. טָוָה
8. טָחָה
9. חָטָא
10. יָד
11. דָּוִד

12. יָחִיד
13. כּוֹבֶד
14. כּוֹכב
15. לֹא
16. לוּחַ
17. לְבַד
18. לָהַט
19. לֶחֶם
20. מַלְאָךְ
21. מֶלֶךְ

1 . הַכּוֹכָב לָהַט מַלְאָךְ .

_____

2 . הָמַלְאָךְ יַהֹוָה מִלְחָמָה לְבַד.

_____

3 . הָכַד הָיָה כּוֹבֶד.

_____

4. הַמֶּלֶךְ דָּוִד מִלְחָמָה הַחָטָא.

_____

5. יַהוֶה הוּא הָיָה אָבִי.

_____

מֶלֶךְ דָּוִד
King David =

•*Nun*
• Sound: **n**

Nun = Seed

Nun is the 14th letter of the Hebrew Aleph-bet. **It is pronounced 'n' as in noon.**

When *Nun* is at the end of a word, a *Nun-Sophit* is used. *Nun-Sophit* has a different shape than a regular *Nun* but the sound is the same.

Nun-Sophit looks like the letter Dalet, **but they extend below the guide-line.**

E-class Vowels:

Hebrew **vowels** are a series of dots or dashes that are placed below or above Hebrew **consonants**.

The next vowel (*niqqud*) makes an e-sound:

Tzere

e as in they

Read Aloud *(Haq'rey)*:
Let's practice reading with *tzere*. *Tzere* **is a vowel with 2 dots underneath a Hebrew letter.** It is pronounced like an 'e' in **they**.

הֵ דֵ גֵ בֵ בֵ אֵ

(hey) (dey) (gey) (vey) (bey) (ey)

לִי אֹכֵא לֵלוֹ הֵלוֹ בֵּגֵל זֵאד

(Zeyd) (Beygel) (Heylo) (Leylo) (Okey) (Ley)

טֵךְ וֵאט חֵךְ טֵדִי בֵּיט

(Beyt) (Tudey) (Kheyk) (Weyt) (Teyk)

Matching Sets:
Let's see how well you know your stuff. Match each English word with the correct Hebrew transliteration``.

Take   אָכֶא

Halo   בְּגֶל

Cake   בֵּיט

Bagel   הֵלוֹ

Okay   טֶדִי

Today   טֶך

Wait   וְאֵט

Bait   חֶך

Prophet = נָבִיא

Prince = נָגִיד

Priest = כּוֹהֵן

Yes = כֵּן
(Keyn)

Give = נָתַן
(Natan) *ת=t

Stretch = נוֹטֶה

1 2 3 4 5 6

ih-eh-uh-oh-ey-ah
1 2 3 4 5 6

Congratulations!!!

You have now learned 6 of the 7 vowel types!

The 7 vowel types are a reflection of the 7 *Spirits* mentioned in the Book of Revelation:

Hebrew Israelite Scriptures

Revelation 1:3 Blessed is he that *readeth*, and they that *hear* the words of this prophecy, and keep those things which are *written* therein: for the time is at hand.

Revelation 1:4 Yokhanan to the seven Assemblies which are in Asia: Grace be unto you, and shalom, from him WHICH IS, and WHICH WAS and WHICH IS TO COME; and from *the seven (7) Spirits* which are before his throne.

The Hebrew Language has 3 parts: *reading*, *speaking* and *writing*. This is mentioned in Rev 1:3 (in order to *hear*, someone else has to *speak*). These 3 parts represent YAHOWAH the *One WHICH IS*, and *WHICH WAS* and *WHICH IS TO COME*.

There are 7 Spirits before the throne of YAH. When YAHOWAH *spoke* creation into existance by His Word, the 7 Spirits became the 7 Vibrations (Vowels) of Hebrew.

• **Samek**

• Sound: **s**

Samek = Support

Samek is the 15th letter of the Hebrew Aleph-bet. **It is pronounced 's' as in song.**

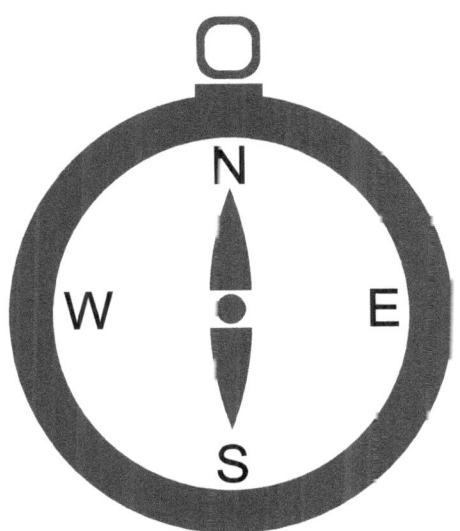

Support = סָמֵךְ

Compass = סָבִיב

Horse = סוּס

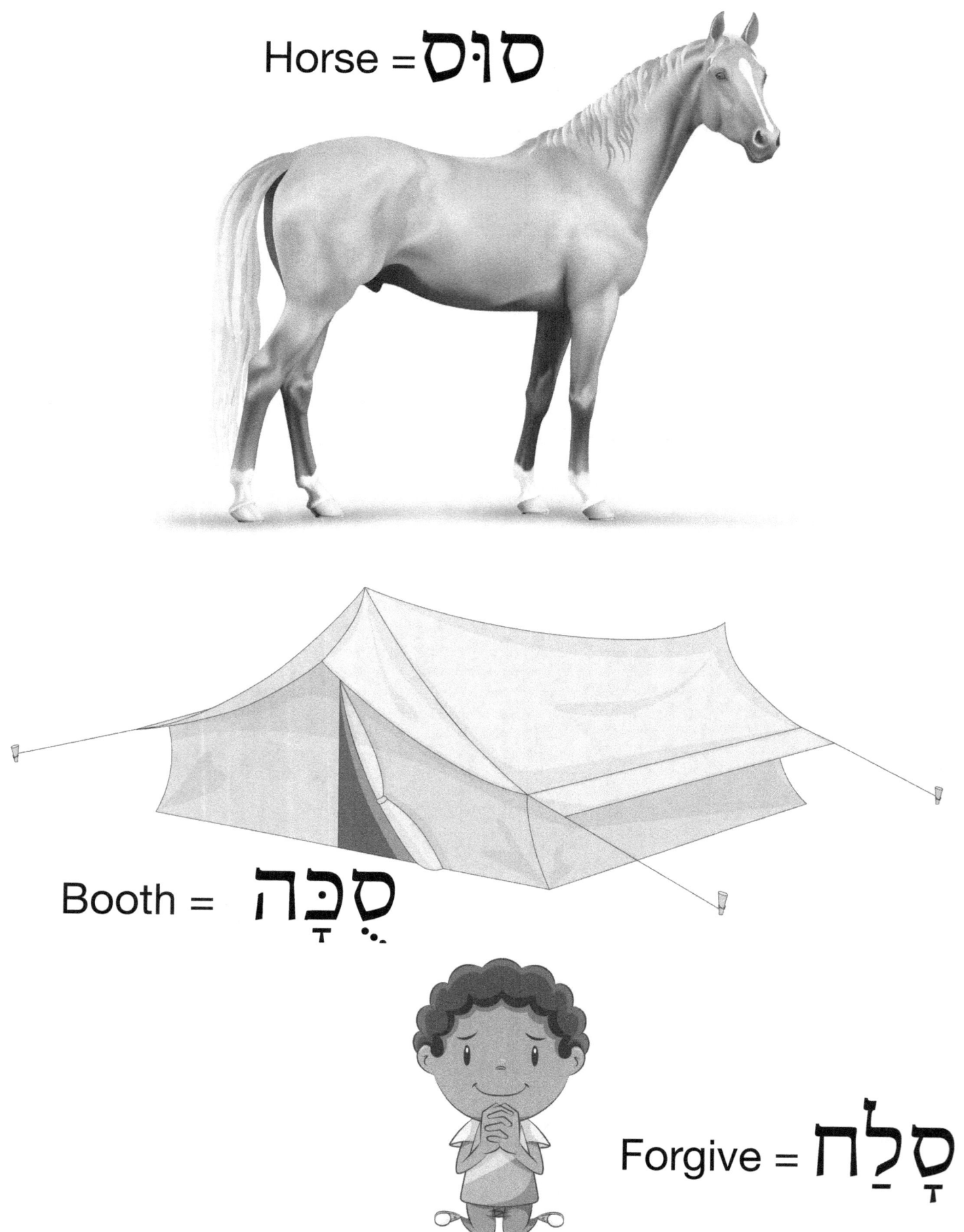

Booth = סֻכָּה

Forgive = סָלַח

Samek and **Mem-Sophit** look very similar. Can you tell the difference between them? Circle each **Samek** below and put a square around each **Mem-Sophit**.

ש	ל	ס	ג	ט	ח	כ
ל	י	א	ר	ע	צ	ת
ק	ם	ו	ס	ת	ף	ס
י	ר	ך	נ	ל	שׂ	נ
נ	ז	כ	ע	ט	מ	ק
ם	צ	ק	ך	ם	ס	י
ס	ע	ת	ג	ל	ת	ם

How many **Sameks** do you see? ___ How many **Mem-Sophits** do you see?

___
Use the number of *Sameks* to find the chapter and the number of *Mem-Sophits* to find this verse:

Proverbs ___:___ *Get wisdom, get understanding: forget it not; neither decline from the words of my mouth.*

• *Ayin*

• Sound: **silent**

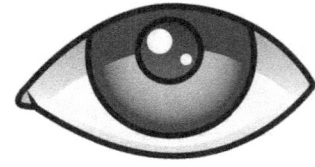

Ayin = Eye

Ayin is the 16th letter of the Hebrew Aleph-bet. It is a **silent letter** that only takes on the sound of an associated vowel symbol.

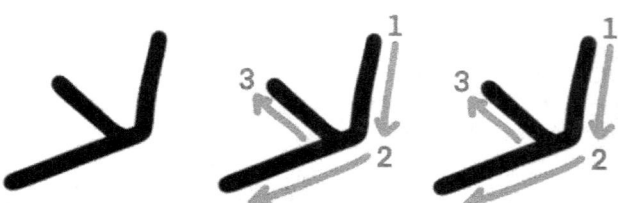

Work = עָבַד

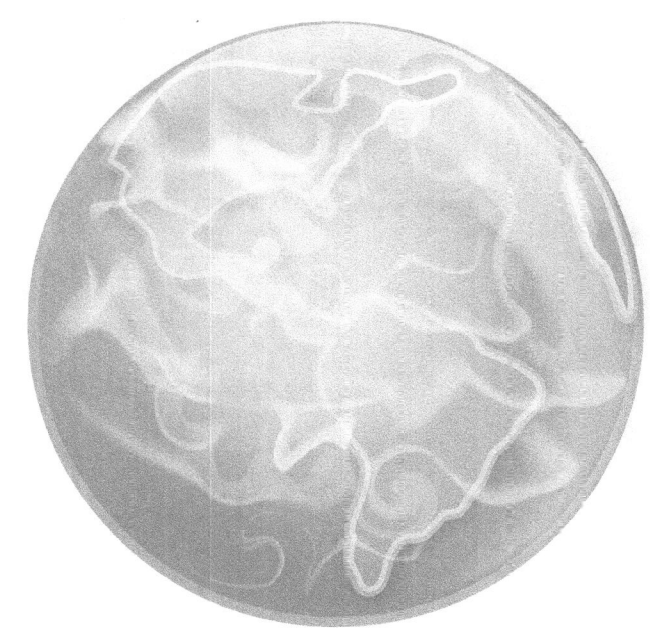

Answered = עָנָה

World = עוֹלָם

Stand = עָמַד

Hebrew Crosswords

Fill in the crossword puzzle in Hebrew by using clues from the english words below.

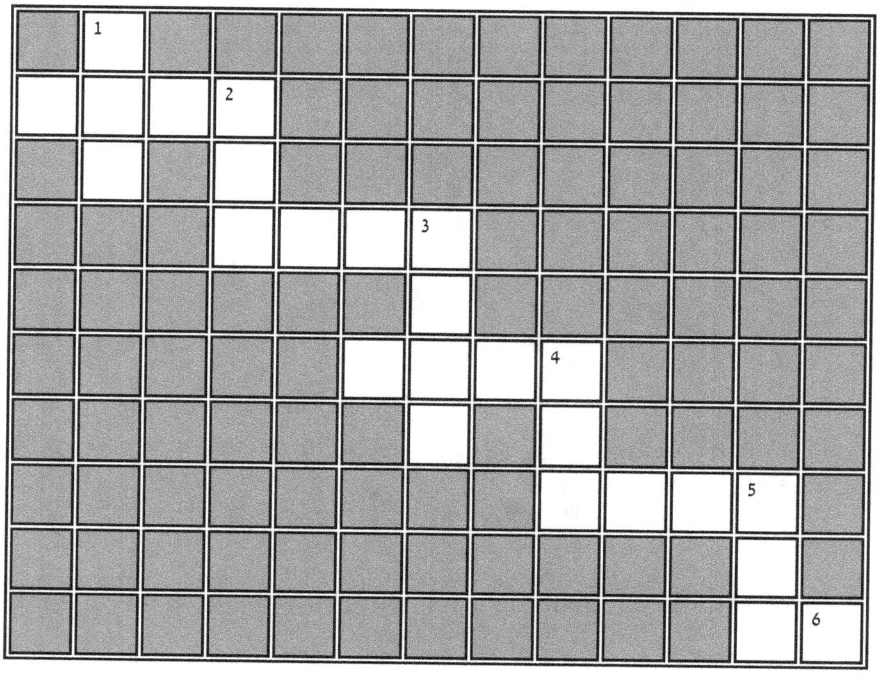

Across

2 World

3 Prince

4 Compass

5 Stretch

6 Yes

Down

1 Forgive

2 Stand

3 Prophet

4 Booth

5 Give

· *Peh*

· Sound: p

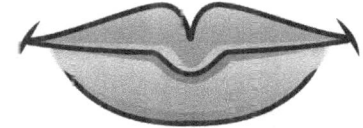

Peh = Mouth

Peh is the 17th letter of the Hebrew Aleph-bet. **It is pronounced 'p' as in pool.**

  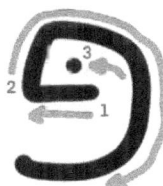

When *Peh* does not have a dot in its center, it is pronounced 'f' as in food.

  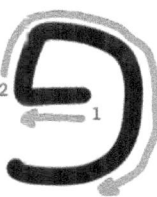

Strike = 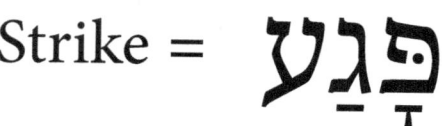 פֶּגַע

Mouth = פֶּה

When **Feh** is at the end of a word, a **Feh-Sophit** is used. **Feh-Sophit** has a different shape than a regular **Feh** but the sound is the same.

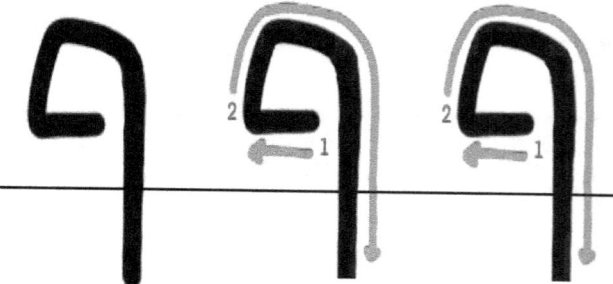

Silver = כֶּסֶף

Payment = פְּעֻלָּה

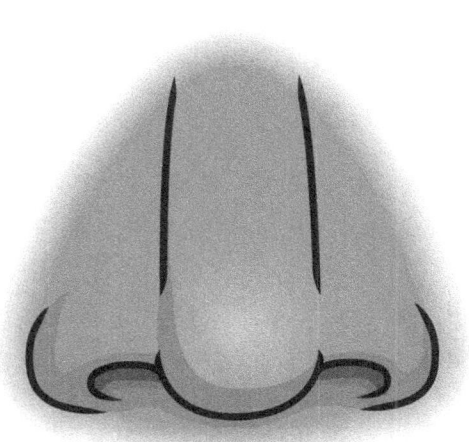

Nose = אַף

Face = פָּנִים
(Panim)

· Tzaday

· Sound: tz

Tzaday = Fish Hook

Tzaday is the 18th letter of the Hebrew Aleph-bet. **It is pronounced 'tz' as in ka**tz**.**

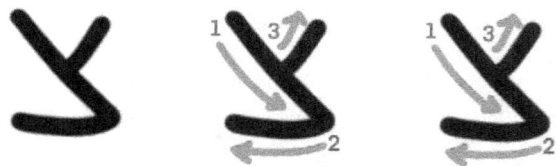

When *Tzaday* is at the end of a word, a *Tzaday-Sophit* is used. *Tzaday-Sophit* has a different shape than a regular *Tzaday* but **the sound is the same.**

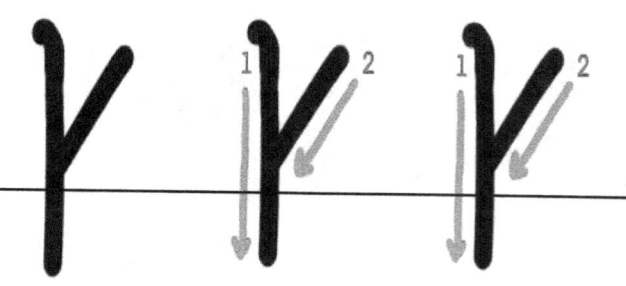

Note: *Tzaday-Sophit* extends below the guide-line.

86

Laugh = צָחֵק
(Tzakhaq)
*ק=q

Hunt = צוּד

FRESH JUICE
natural product

Juice = מִיץ
(Meetz)

Tree = עֵץ

Deer = צְבִי
(Tz'vi)

1 . אָחִי הוּא צוּד הַצְבִי .

_____

2 . יַהְוֶה הוּא סָלַח מֶלֶךְ דָוִד.

_____

3 . הַמַלְאַךְ יַהְוֶה סָמַךְ אָבִי.

_____

כ מ נ פ צ

ך ס ו ף ץ

Kaph-Sophit

Mem-Sophit

Nun-Sophit

Peh-Sophit

Tzaday Sophit

Congratulations!!!

You have now learned all 5 *sophit* (final-form) letters!

ק **· Qoof**

· Sound: q

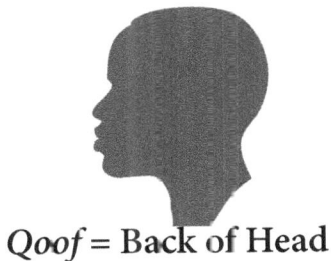

Qoof = Back of Head

Qoof is the 19th letter of the Hebrew Aleph-bet. **It is pronounced 'q' as in q**uick.

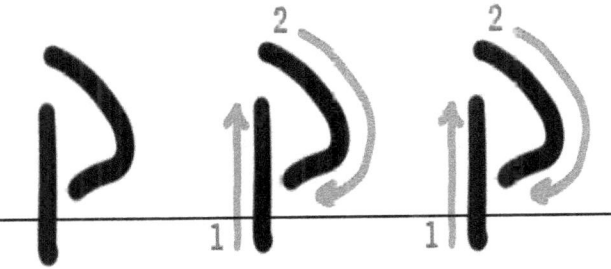

Ancient = קֶדֶם

Rise = קוּם

Receive = קָבֵּל

Assembly = קָהֵל

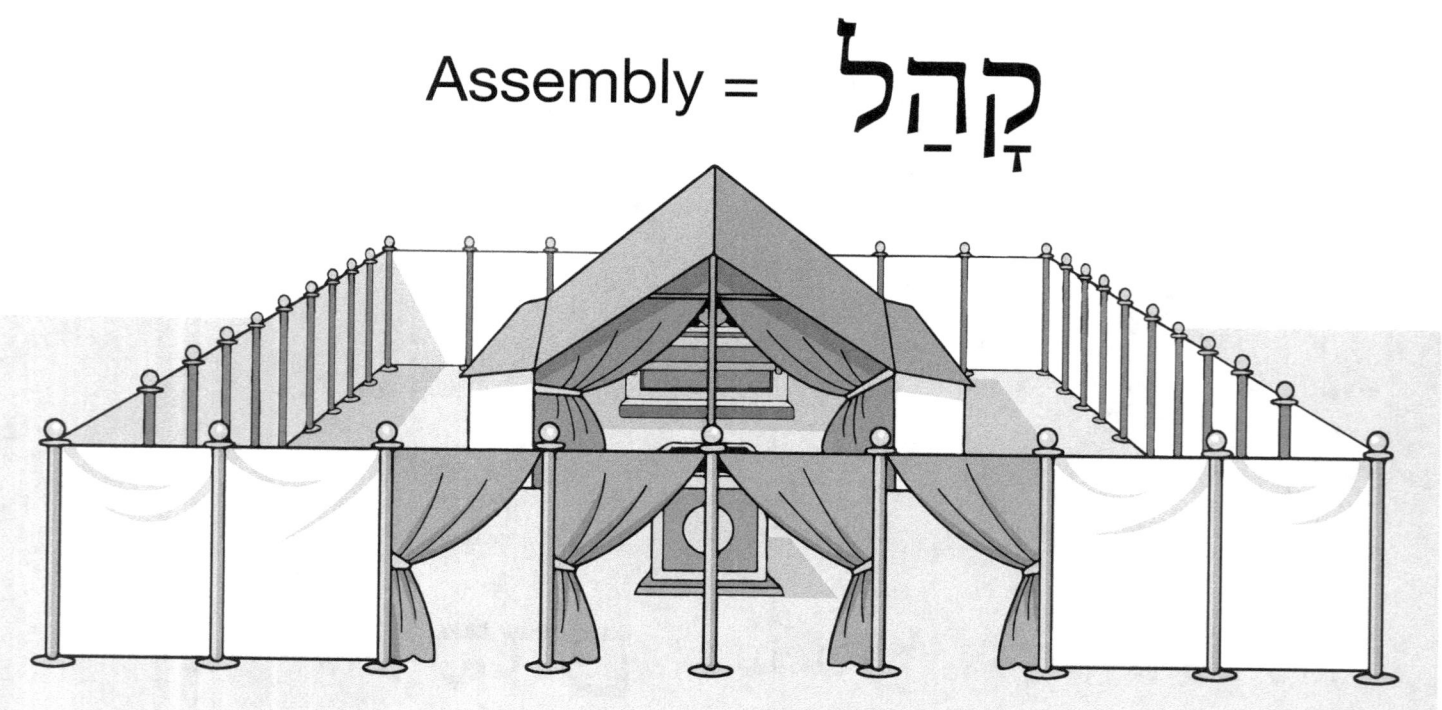

1. The ancient Assembly recieved the Angel.

_____

2. The horse answered the prince.

_____

3. The priest he worked the Assembly.

_____

ר

• Resh
• Sound: r

Resh = Head

Resh is the 20th letter of the Hebrew Aleph-bet. **It is pronounced 'r' as in run.**

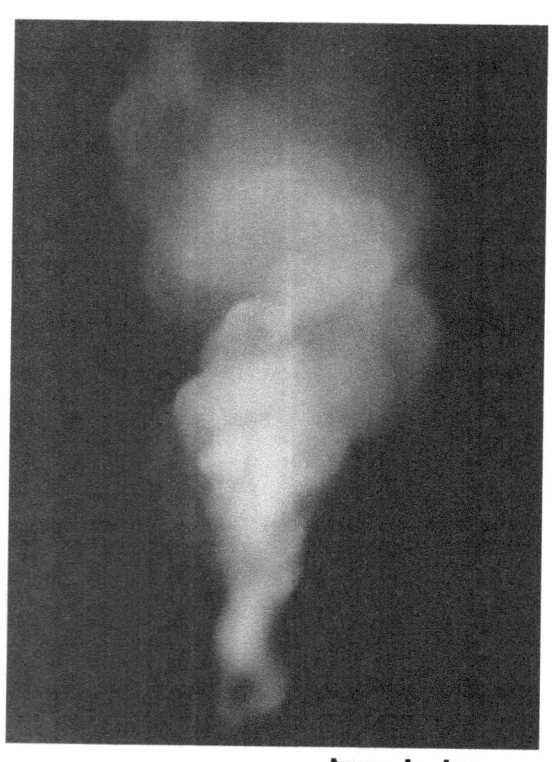

Spirit = רוּחַ
(Ruakh)

Leg = רֶגֶל

Doctor = רוֹפֵא

See = רוֹאֶה

Want = רָצָה

1. הָרוֹפֵא הוּא רָאַה הַנָּבִיא .

_____

2. כֵּן הַפְּעֻלָּה הַמֶּלֶךְ רָצָה הָיָה
כֶּסֶף.

_____

3. הָרוּחַ יַהֲוֶה הָיָה קֶדֶם.

_____

· *Sheen*

· Sound: **sh**

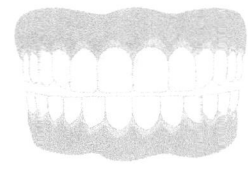

Sheen = Teeth

Sheen is the 21th letter of the Hebrew Aleph-bet. **When** *Sheen* **has a** dot **over the** right side **it is pronounced 'sh' as in** short.

When *Seen* **has a** dot **over the** left side **it is pronounced 's' as in** sun.

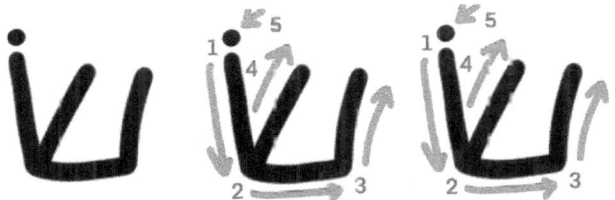

Peace = שָׁלוֹם

Rejoice = שָׂמֵחַ

Sing = שִׁיר

98

Field = שָׂדֶה

Put = שִׂים
(Siym)

Lay = שָׁכַב

Name: _____

Hebrew Word Search

Find the hidden english words by using clues from the Hebrew words below.

```
C  G  H  T  P  R  I  S  I  L  V  E  R  G  D  A  M  D
F  B  A  R  H  T  R  E  E  K  L  N  Z  N  R  T  A  F
A  U  E  C  M  O  U  T  H  C  Z  A  A  I  Y  T  C  R
V  E  H  U  N  T  E  L  V  P  J  T  U  S  C  T  M  E
D  F  W  O  R  R  C  N  R  A  U  T  L  G  S  N  D  C
U  H  Y  C  Z  E  I  E  F  N  N  T  N  E  H  E  F  E
D  Y  E  A  G  J  U  K  A  P  N  C  I  A  G  M  I  I
O  A  V  V  L  O  J  I  C  L  N  M  I  R  W  Y  E  V
C  S  E  E  R  I  Q  R  E  I  S  O  E  E  I  A  L  E
T  H  T  I  I  C  U  T  D  Y  Q  K  S  P  N  P  D  Y
O  K  S  U  O  E  B  S  P  E  A  C  E  E  L  T  S  C
R  E  D  J  P  L  W  K  O  S  A  S  S  E  M  B  L  Y
```

1. פֶּגַע
2. פֶּה
3. כֶּסֶף
4. פְּעֻלָּה
5. אַף
6. פָּנִים
7. צוּד
8. צָחַק
9. מִיץ
10. עֵץ
11. צְבִי
12. קֶדֶם
13. קוּם

14. קִבֵּל
15. קָהָל
16. רֶגֶל
17. רוּחַ
18. רוֹפֵא
19. רוֹאֶה
20. רָצָה
21. שָׁלוֹם
22. שָׂמַח
23. שִׁיר
24. שָׂדֶה
25. שִׂים
26. שָׁכַב

• *Taw*
• Sound: **t**

Taw = The Cross

Taw is the 22th letter of the Hebrew Aleph-bet. **It is pronounced 't' as in** touch. *Taw* **has a dot (dagesh) in it when it is at the beginning of a word but the sound is still the same.**

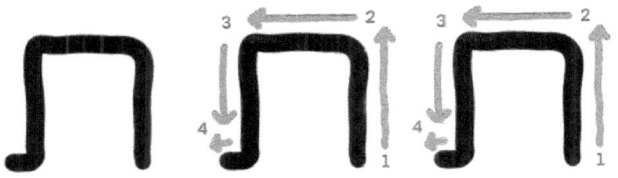

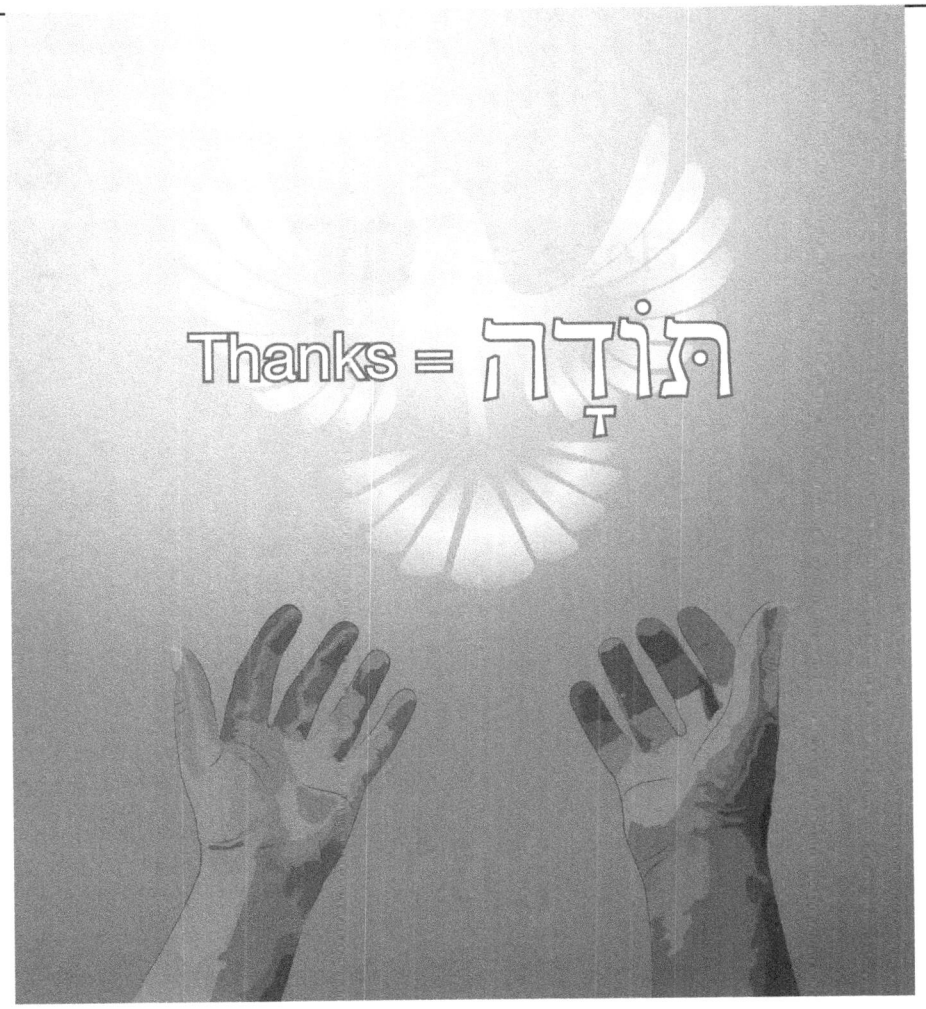

Thanks = תּוֹדָה

Law =

תּוֹרָה

Hope = תִּקְוָה

Picture = תְּמוּנָה

Name: _____

Hebrew Word Search

Find the hidden english words by using clues from the Hebrew words below.

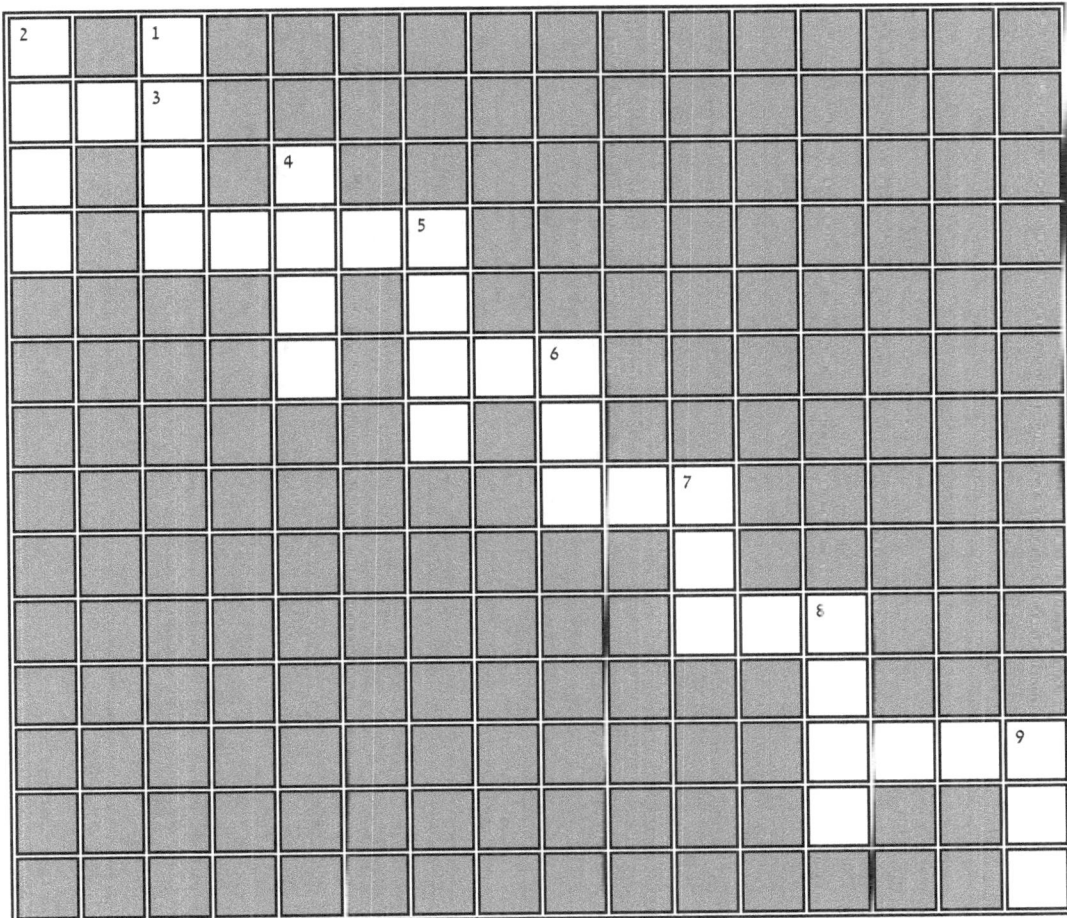

Across		Down	
3	Receive	1	Hope
5	Picture	2	Peace
6	Sing	4	Thanks
7	Ancient	5	Law
8	Leg	6	Put
9	Doctor	7	Assembly
		8	See
		9	Want

Congratulations!!!

You have now learned all 22 (את) letters of the *Alephbet*!

Revelation 1:8 I am *Aleph* and *Taw* (**את**), saith YAHOWAH, WHICH IS, and WHICH WAS and WHICH IS TO COME, the Almighty.

Did You Know???

- The Old and New Testaments are 66 books = 22 (את) x 3

- There are 22 (את) chapters in the book of Revelation.

- There are 22 (את) generations from Adam-Ya'aqob.

- There are 22 (את) epistles in the New Covenant

- **YAHOWAH** created 22 (את) different works until the 7th day.

- **YAHOSHUA** quoted from Psalms 22 (את) before He was crucified.

- When the Tabernacle of Mosheh was completed, there were 22 (את) thousand Levites consecrated to serve.

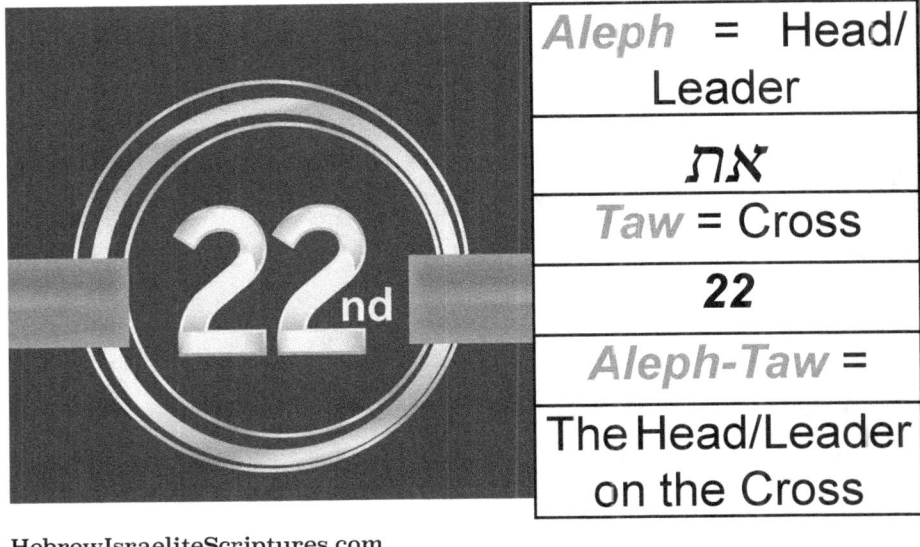

Aleph = Head/Leader	
את	
Taw = Cross	
22	
Aleph-Taw =	
The Head/Leader on the Cross	

The *7th* **Vowel Type:** *Yod-Combinations*

This next vowel combination makes a long i-sound:

Qamatz-*Yod* / **Patakh-***Yod*

i as in ice
ai as in Thai

Whenever a *qamatz* or *patakh* is immediately followed by a *yod*, the vowel changes from an *'a'* as in *about* to a long *'i'* as in *ice* or *'ai'* as in *Thai*.

Read Aloud *(Haq'rey)*:
Let's practice reading with *qamatz-yod* and *patakh-yod*. *Qamatz-yod* and *patakh-yod* are pronounced like an *'i'* as in ice or *'ai'* as in Thai.

חַי לִי וַי הָי דַי גַי בֵּי אָי
(khai) *(lai)* *(wai)* *(hai)* *(dai)* *(gai)* *(bai)* *(ai)*

שָׂדַי בָּנַי אַבְתַי אֱלֹהַי שָׂרַי

יָדַיִם מִצְרַיִם שָׂמַיִם הַמַּיִם

Congratulations!!!

You have now learned the 7th Vowel Type: The Yod-Combinations. Yod can also be combined as follows:

וֹי	'oy' as in boy	גּוֹי	goy
וּי	'uey' as in gluey	רָאוּי	ra'uey
אִיו*	'aiw' as in Taiwan	אֱלֹהָיו	Elohaiw
*The black Aleph is just used as a place holder for any letter.			

Hebrew Words & Phrases

דְּבָרִים וְבִּיטוּיִים בְּעִבְרִית

(D'barim w'Bituyim b'Ivrit)

People & Family

I	אֲנִי	Father	אָב
You (m)	אַתָּה	Mother	אֵם
You (f)	אַתְּ	Brother	אָח
He	הוּא	Sister	אָחוֹת
She	הִיא	Son	בֵּן
We	אֲנַחְנוּ	Daughter	בַּת
You (mp)	אַתֶּם	Grandfather	סָבָא
You (fp)	אַתֶּן	Grandmother	סַבְתָּא
They (mp)	הֵם	Uncle	דּוֹד
They (fp)	הֵן	Aunt	דּוֹדה
Him	אוֹתוֹ	Cousin (m)	דּוֹדָן
Her	אוֹתה	Cousin (f)	דּוֹדנית
Us	אוֹתנו	Husband	אִישׁ
		Wife	אִשָּׁה

Hebrew Greetings

Hello	שָׁלוֹם
How are you? (m)	מַה שְׁלוֹמְךָ?
How are you? (f)	מַה שְׁלוֹמֵךְ?
I am well (m)	אֲנִי טוֹב
I am well (f)	אֲנִי טוֹבה
What's your name?	מַה שְׁמֵךְ? (שְׁמֵךְ?)
My name is...	שְׁמִי ...
How was your day? (m)	אֵיךְ הָיָה יוֹמְךָ?
How was your day? (f)	אֵיךְ הָיָה יוֹמֵךְ?
My day was fine.	יוֹמִי הָיָה טוֹב
I love you (m)	אֲנִי אוֹהֵב אוֹתְךָ
I love you (f)	אֲנִי אוֹהֶבֶת אוֹתֵךְ
Forgive me/Excuse me	סְלַח לִי
Please	בְּבַקָשָׁה
Thank you	תּוֹדָה
You're welcome	אֵין דְבַר
I want (m)	אֲנִי רוֹצֶה ...
I want (f)	אֲנִי רוֹצָה ...
What are you doing? (m)	מַה אַתָּה עוֹשֶׂה?
What are you doing?	מַה אַתְּ עוֹשָׂה?
See you later	לְהִתְרָאוֹת
Good morning	בּוֹקֶר טוֹב
Good night	לַיְלָה טוֹב

Questions & Days of the Week

Who?	מִי?
What?	מַה?
When?	מָתַי?
Where?	אֵיפֹה?
Why?	מַדוּעַ
How?	אֵיךְ?
How much?	כַּמָה?
Sunday	יוֹם רִאשׁוֹן
Monday	יוֹם שֵׁנִי
Tuesday	יוֹם שְׁלִישִׁי
Wednesday	יוֹם רְבִיעִי
Thursday	יוֹם חֲמִישִׁי
Friday	יוֹם שִׁישִׁי
Sabbath	יוֹם שַׁבָּת
My	שֶׁלִי
Your (m)	שֶׁלְךָ
Your (f)	שֶׁלָךְ
His	שֶׁלוֹ
Her	שֶׁלָה
Our	שֶׁלָנוּ
Their (m)	שֶׁלָהֶם
Their (f)	שֶׁלָהֶן

English Numeral	Hebrew Numeral	Hebrew Symbol
0	אֶפֶס	
1	אַחַת	א
2	שְׁתַּיִם	ב
3	שָׁלוֹשׁ	ג
4	אַרְבַּע	ד
5	חָמֵשׁ	ה
6	שֵׁשׁ	ו
7	שֶׁבַע	ז
8	שְׁמוֹנֶה	ח
9	תֵּשַׁע	ט
10	עֶשֶׂר	י
11	אַחַת עֶשְׂרֵה	יא
12	שְׁתֵּים עֶשְׂרֵה	יב
13	שְׁלוֹשׁ עֶשְׂרֵה	יג
14	אַרְבַּע עֶשְׂרֵה	יד
15	חֲמֵשׁ עֶשְׂרֵה	טו
16	שֵׁשׁ עֶשְׂרֵה	טז
17	שְׁבַע עֶשְׂרֵה	יז
18	שְׁמוֹנֶה עֶשְׂרֵה	יח
19	תְּשַׁע עֶשְׂרֵה	יט
20	עֶשְׂרִים	כ

ל-30 מ-40 נ-50 ס-60 ע-70 פ-80 צ-90

ק-100 ר-200 ש-300 ת-400

Hebrew Reading Practice

קְרִיאָה תַּרְגִיל

(Q'riy'ah Targil)

The Priestly Blessing (Numbers 6:23-27)

23 דַּבֵּר אֶל-אַהֲרֹן וְאֶל-בָּנָיו לֵאמֹר, כֹּה תְבָרְכוּ אֶת-בְּנֵי
יִשְׂרָאֵל: אָמוֹר, לָהֶם.

24 יְבָרֶכְךָ יְהוָה, וְיִשְׁמְרֶךָ.

25 יָאֵר יְהוָה פָּנָיו אֵלֶיךָ, וִיחֻנֶּךָּ.

26 יִשָּׂא יְהוָה פָּנָיו אֵלֶיךָ, וְיָשֵׂם לְךָ שָׁלוֹם.

27 וְשָׂמוּ אֶת-שְׁמִי, עַל-בְּנֵי יִשְׂרָאֵל; וַאֲנִי, אֲבָרְכֵם.

23 Speak unto Aharon and unto his sons, saying, On this wise ye shall bless the children of Yisra'EL, saying unto them,

24 YAHOWAH bless thee, and keep thee:

25 YAHOWAH make his face shine upon thee, and be gracious unto thee:

26 YAHOWAH lift up his countenance upon thee, and give thee shalom.

27 And they shall put my name upon the children of Yisra'EL; and I will bless them.

Psalm 150

1 הַלְלוּ־יָהּ: הַלְלוּ־אֵל בְּקָדְשׁוֹ; הַלְלוּהוּ, בִּרְקִיעַ עֻזּוֹ.

2 הַלְלוּהוּ בִגְבוּרֹתָיו; הַלְלוּהוּ, כְּרֹב גֻּדְלוֹ.

3 הַלְלוּהוּ, בְּתֵקַע שׁוֹפָר; הַלְלוּהוּ, בְּנֵבֶל וְכִנּוֹר.

4 הַלְלוּהוּ, בְּתֹף וּמָחוֹל; הַלְלוּהוּ, בְּמִנִּים וְעֻגָב.

5 הַלְלוּהוּ בְצִלְצְלֵי־שָׁמַע; הַלְלוּהוּ, בְּצִלְצְלֵי תְרוּעָה.

6 כֹּל הַנְּשָׁמָה, תְּהַלֵּל יָהּ: הַלְלוּ־יָהּ.

1 HalleluYah! Praise Elohim in his sanctuary: praise him in the firmament of his power.
2 Praise him for his mighty acts: praise him according to his excellent greatness.
3 Praise him with the sound of the trumpet: praise him with the psaltery and harp.
4 Praise him with the timbrel and dance: praise him with stringed instruments and organs.
5 Praise him upon the loud cymbals: praise him upon the high sounding cymbals.
6 Let every thing that hath breath praise Yah.
HalleluYah!

Reading Practice

King Solomon's Prayer A (1 Kings 8:15-21)

15 וַיֹּאמֶר, בָּרוּךְ *יַהֲוֶה* אֱלֹהֵי יִשְׂרָאֵל, אֲשֶׁר דִּבֶּר בְּפִיו, אֵת דָּוִד אָבִי; וּבְיָדוֹ מִלֵּא, לֵאמֹר.

16 מִן-הַיּוֹם, אֲשֶׁר הוֹצֵאתִי אֶת-עַמִּי אֶת-יִשְׂרָאֵל מִמִּצְרַיִם, לֹא-בָחַרְתִּי בְעִיר מִכֹּל שִׁבְטֵי יִשְׂרָאֵל, לִבְנוֹת בַּיִת לִהְיוֹת שְׁמִי שָׁם; וָאֶבְחַר בְּדָוִד, לִהְיוֹת עַל-עַמִּי יִשְׂרָאֵל.

17 וַיְהִי, עִם-לְבַב דָּוִד אָבִי--לִבְנוֹת בַּיִת, לְשֵׁם *יַהֲוֶה* אֱלֹהֵי יִשְׂרָאֵל.

18 וַיֹּאמֶר *יַהֲוֶה*, אֶל-דָּוִד אָבִי, יַעַן אֲשֶׁר הָיָה עִם-לְבָבְךָ, לִבְנוֹת בַּיִת לִשְׁמִי--הֱטִיבֹתָ, כִּי הָיָה עִם-לְבָבֶךָ.

19 רַק אַתָּה, לֹא תִבְנֶה הַבָּיִת: כִּי אִם-בִּנְךָ הַיֹּצֵא מֵחֲלָצֶיךָ, הוּא-יִבְנֶה הַבַּיִת לִשְׁמִי.

20 וַיָּקֶם *יַהֲוֶה*, אֶת-דְּבָרוֹ אֲשֶׁר דִּבֵּר; וָאָקֻם תַּחַת דָּוִד אָבִי וָאֵשֵׁב עַל-כִּסֵּא יִשְׂרָאֵל, כַּאֲשֶׁר דִּבֶּר *יַהֲוֶה*, וָאֶבְנֶה הַבַּיִת, לְשֵׁם *יַהֲוֶה* אֱלֹהֵי יִשְׂרָאֵל.

21 וָאָשִׂם שָׁם מָקוֹם לָאָרוֹן, אֲשֶׁר-שָׁם בְּרִית *יַהֲוֶה*, אֲשֶׁר כָּרַת עִם-אֲבֹתֵינוּ, בְּהוֹצִיאוֹ אֹתָם מֵאֶרֶץ מִצְרָיִם.

READING PRACTICE

King Solomon's Prayer A (1 Kings 8:15-21)

15 And he said, Blessed be YAHOWAH ELOHIM of Yisra'EL, which spake with his mouth unto Dawid my father, and hath with his hand fulfilled it, saying,

16 Since the day that I brought forth my people Yisra'EL out of Mitzraim, I chose no city out of all the tribes of Yisra'EL to build an house, that my name might be therein; but I chose Dawid
to be over my people Yisra'EL.

17 And it was in the heart of Dawid my father to build an house for the name of YAHOWAH ELOHIM of Yisra'EL.

18 And YAHOWAH said unto Dawid my father, Whereas it was in thine heart to build an house unto my name, thou didst well that it was in thine heart.

19 Nevertheless thou shalt not build the house; but thy son that shall come forth out of thy loins, he shall build the house unto my name.

20 And YAHOWAH hath performed his word that he spake, and I am risen up in the room of Dawid my father, and sit on the throne of Yisra'EL, as YAHOWAH promised, and have built an house for the name of YAHOWAH ELOHIM of Yisra'EL.

21 And I have set there a place for the ark, wherein is the covenant of YAHOWAH, which he made with our fathers, when he brought them out of the land of Mitzraim.

Reading Practice

King Solomon's Prayer B (1 Kings 8:25-30)

25 וְעַתָּה *יַהְוֶה* אֱלֹהֵי יִשְׂרָאֵל, שְׁמֹר לְעַבְדְּךָ דָוִד אָבִי אֵת אֲשֶׁר דִּבַּרְתָּ לּוֹ לֵאמֹר, לֹא-יִכָּרֵת לְךָ אִישׁ מִלְּפָנַי, יֹשֵׁב עַל-כִּסֵּא יִשְׂרָאֵל: רַק אִם-יִשְׁמְרוּ בָנֶיךָ אֶת-דַּרְכָּם, לָלֶכֶת לְפָנַי, כַּאֲשֶׁר הָלַכְתָּ, לְפָנָי.

26 וְעַתָּה, אֱלֹהֵי יִשְׂרָאֵל--יֵאָמֶן נָא, דבריך (דְּבָרְךָ), אֲשֶׁר דִּבַּרְתָּ, לְעַבְדְּךָ דָוִד אָבִי.

27 כִּי, הַאֻמְנָם, יֵשֵׁב אֱלֹהִים, עַל-הָאָרֶץ; הִנֵּה הַשָּׁמַיִם וּשְׁמֵי הַשָּׁמַיִם, לֹא יְכַלְכְּלוּךָ--אַף, כִּי-הַבַּיִת הַזֶּה אֲשֶׁר בָּנִיתִי.

28 וּפָנִיתָ אֶל-תְּפִלַּת עַבְדְּךָ, וְאֶל-תְּחִנָּתוֹ--*יַהְוֶה* אֱלֹהָי: לִשְׁמֹעַ אֶל-הָרִנָּה וְאֶל-הַתְּפִלָּה, אֲשֶׁר עַבְדְּךָ מִתְפַּלֵּל לְפָנֶיךָ הַיּוֹם.

29 לִהְיוֹת עֵינֶךָ פְתֻחֹת אֶל-הַבַּיִת הַזֶּה, לַיְלָה וָיוֹם, אֶל-הַמָּקוֹם, אֲשֶׁר אָמַרְתָּ יִהְיֶה שְׁמִי שָׁם--לִשְׁמֹעַ, אֶל-הַתְּפִלָּה, אֲשֶׁר יִתְפַּלֵּל עַבְדְּךָ, אֶל-הַמָּקוֹם הַזֶּה.

30 וְשָׁמַעְתָּ אֶל-תְּחִנַּת עַבְדְּךָ, וְעַמְּךָ יִשְׂרָאֵל, אֲשֶׁר יִתְפַּלְלוּ, אֶל-הַמָּקוֹם הַזֶּה; וְאַתָּה תִּשְׁמַע אֶל-מְקוֹם שִׁבְתְּךָ, אֶל-הַשָּׁמַיִם, וְשָׁמַעְתָּ, וְסָלָחְתָּ.

READING PRACTICE

King Solomon's Prayer B (1 Kings 8:25-30)

25 Therefore now, YAHOWAH ELOHIM of Yisra'EL, keep with thy servant Dawid my father that thou promisedst him, saying: There shall not fail thee a man in my sight to sit on the throne of Yisra'EL; so that thy children take heed to their way, that they walk before me as thou hast walked before me.

26 And now, O ELOHIM of Yisra'EL, let thy word, I pray thee, be verified, which thou spakest unto thy servant Dawid my father.

27 But will ELOHIM indeed dwell on the earth? behold, the heaven and heaven of heavens cannot contain thee; how much less this house that I have builded?

28 Yet have thou respect unto the prayer of thy servant, and to his supplication, O YAHOWAH my ELOHIM, to hearken unto the cry and to the prayer, which thy servant prayeth before thee to day:

29 That thine eyes may be open toward this house night and day, even toward the place of which thou hast said, My name shall be there: that thou mayest hearken unto the prayer which thy servant shall make toward this place.

30 And hearken thou to the supplication of thy servant, and of thy people Yisra'EL, when they shall pray toward this place: and hear thou in heaven thy dwelling place: and when thou hearest, forgive.

READING PRACTICE

In The Beginning Was The Word (John 1:1-12)

1 בְּרֵאשִׁית הָיָה הַדָּבָר וְהַדָּבָר הָיָה אֵת הָאֱלֹהִים וֵאלֹהִים
הָיָה הַדָּבָר:

2 הוּא הָיָה בְּרֵאשִׁית אֵת הָאֱלֹהִים:

3 הַכֹּל נִהְיָה עַל־יָדוֹ וּמִבַּלְעָדָיו לֹא נִהְיָה כָּל־אֲשֶׁר נִהְיָה:

4 בּוֹ הָיוּ חַיִּים וְהַחַיִּים הָיוּ אוֹר לִבְנֵי הָאָדָם:

5 וְהָאוֹר הֵאִיר בַּחֹשֶׁךְ וְהַחֹשֶׁךְ לֹא הִשִּׂיגוֹ:

6 וַיְהִי אִישׁ שָׁלוּחַ מֵאֵת הָאֱלֹהִים שׁוּמוֹ יוֹחָנָן:

7 הוּא בָּא לְעֵדוּת לְהָעִיד עַל־הָאוֹר לְמַעַן יַאֲמִינוּ כֻלָּם עַל־
יָדוֹ:

8 הוּא לֹא־הָיָה הָאוֹר כִּי אִם־לְהָעִיד עַל־הָאוֹר:

9 הָאוֹר הָאֲמִתִּי הַמֵּאִיר לְכָל־אָדָם אֲשֶׁר בָּא אֶל־הָעוֹלָם:

10 בָּעוֹלָם הָיָה וְעַל־יָדוֹ נִהְיָה הָעוֹלָם וְהָעוֹלָם לֹא יְדָעוֹ:

11 וְהוּא בָּא בְּשֶׁלּוֹ וַאֲשֶׁר־הֵמָּה לוֹ לֹא קִבְּלֻהוּ:

12 וְהַמְקַבְּלִים אֹתוֹ הַמַּאֲמִינִים בִּשְׁמוֹ נָתַן־עֹז לָמוֹ לִהְיוֹת
בָּנִים לֵאלֹהִים:

READING PRACTICE

In The Beginning Was The Word (John 1:1-12)

1 In the beginning was the Word, and the Word was with ELOHIM, and the Word was ELOHIM.

2 The same was in the beginning with ELOHIM.

3 All things were made by him; and without him was not any thing made that was made.

4 In him was life; and the life was the light of men.

5 And the light shineth in darkness; and the darkness comprehended it not.

6 There was a man sent from ELOHIM, whose name was Yokhanan.

7 The same came for a witness, to bear witness of the Light, that all men through him might believe.

8 He was not that Light, but was sent to bear witness of that Light.

9 That was the true Light, which lighteth every man that cometh into the world.

10 He was in the world, and the world was made by him, and the world knew him not.

11 He came unto his own, and his own received him not.

12 But as many as received him, to them gave he power to become the sons of ELOHIM, even to them that believe on his name:

READING PRACTICE

The High Priestly Prayer (John 17:1-10)

1 אֶת־אֵלֶּה דִּבֶּר *יַהוֹשֻׁעַ* וַיִּשָּׂא עֵינָיו הַשָּׁמַיְמָה וַיֹּאמַר אָבִי
הִנֵּה־בָאָה הַשָּׁעָה פָּאֵר אֶת־בִּנְךָ לְמַעַן יְפָאֶרְךָ גַּם־בִּנֶךָ:

2 כַּאֲשֶׁר נָתַתָּ לּוֹ הַשָּׁלְטָן עַל־כָּל־בָּשָׂר לְמַעַן יִתֵּן חַיֵּי עוֹלָם
לְכֹל אֲשֶׁר־נָתַתָּ לּוֹ:

3 וְאֵלֶּה הֵם חַיֵּי הָעוֹלָם לָדַעַת כִּי אַתָּה הָאֱלֹהִים
לְבַדֶּךָ וְאֶת־ *יַהוֹשֻׁעַ הַמָּשִׁיחַ* אֲשֶׁר שָׁלָחְתָּ:

4 אֲנִי פֵאַרְתִּיךָ בָאָרֶץ כִּלִּיתִי מְלַאכְתְּךָ אֲשֶׁר צִוִּיתַנִי לַעֲשׂוֹת:

5 וְעַתָּה פָאֲרֵנִי אַתָּה אָבִי עִמֶּךָ בַּכָּבוֹד אֲשֶׁר הָיָה־לִי עִמְּךָ
טֶרֶם הֱיוֹת הָעוֹלָם:

6 אֶת שִׁמְךָ הוֹדַעְתִּי לִבְנֵי הָאָדָם אֲשֶׁר נָתַתָּ לִי מִתּוֹךְ הָעוֹלָם
לְךָ הָיוּ וְלִי נָתַתָּ אֹתָם וְאֶת־דְּבָרְךָ נָצָרוּ:

7 וְעַתָּה יָדְעוּ כִּי־כֹל אֲשֶׁר נָתַתָּ לִי מֵעִמְּךָ הוּא:

8 כִּי הַדְּבָרִים אֲשֶׁר נָתַתָּ לִי נָתַתִּי לָהֶם וְהֵם קִבְּלוּם וַיַּכִּירוּ
בֶּאֱמֶת כִּי מֵעִמְּךָ יָצָאתִי וַיַּאֲמִינוּ כִּי אַתָּה שְׁלַחְתָּנִי:

9 אֲנִי בַּעֲדָם אַעְתִּיר לָךְ לֹא בְּעַד הָעוֹלָם אַעְתִּיר כִּי אִם־
בְּעַד אֵלֶּה אֲשֶׁר נָתַתָּ לִי כִּי־לְךָ הֵמָּה:

10 וְכָל־אֲשֶׁר לִי לְךָ הוּא וְשֶׁלְּךָ שֶׁלִּי וְנִתְפָּאַרְתִּי בָהֶם:

Reading Practice

The High Priestly Prayer (John 17:1-10)

1 These words spake Yahoshua, and lifted up his eyes to heaven, and said, Father, the hour is come; glorify thy Son, that thy Son also may glorify thee:

2 As thou hast given him power over all flesh, that he should give eternal life to as many as thou hast given him.

3 And this is life eternal, that they might know thee the only true Elohim, and Yahoshua Ha' Mashiakh, whom thou hast sent.

4 I have glorified thee on the earth: I have finished the work which thou gavest me to do.

5 And now, O Father, glorify thou me with thine own self with the glory which I had with thee before the world was.

6 I have manifested thy name unto the men which thou gavest me out of the world: thine they were, and thou gavest them me; and they have kept thy word.

7 Now they have known that all things whatsoever thou hast given me are of thee.

8 For I have given unto them the words which thou gavest me; and they have received them, and have known surely that I came out from thee, and they have believed that thou didst send me.

9 I pray for them: I pray not for the world, but for them which thou hast given me; for they are thine.

10 And all mine are thine, and thine are mine; and I am glorified in them.

11 וַאֲנִי אֵינֶנִּי עוֹד בָּעוֹלָם וְהֵם בָּעוֹלָם הֵמָּה וַאֲנִי בָא אֵלֶיךָ אָבִי הַקָּדוֹשׁ נְצֹר אֹתָם בְּשִׁמְךָ אֶת־אֲשֶׁר נָתַתָּ לִי לְמַעַן יִהְיוּ אֶחָד כְּמֹנוּ:

12 בִּהְיוֹתִי עִמָּהֶם בָּעוֹלָם אֲנִי נָצַרְתִּי אֹתָם בְּשִׁמְךָ אֶת־אֲשֶׁר נָתַתָּם לִי שָׁמַרְתִּי וְלֹא־אָבַד מֵהֶם אִישׁ זוּלָתִי בֶּן־הָאֲבַדּוֹן לְמַלֹּאת דְּבַר הַכָּתוּב:

13 וְעַתָּה הִנְנִי בָא אֵלֶיךָ וְאֶת־אֵלֶּה אֲנִי מְדַבֵּר בָּעוֹלָם לְמַעַן תִּמָּלֵא לָהֶם שִׂמְחָתִי בְּקִרְבָּם:

14 אֲנִי נָתַתִּי לָהֶם אֶת־דְּבָרֶךָ וְהָעוֹלָם שָׂנֵא אֹתָם יַעַן כִּי לֹא מִן־הָעוֹלָם הֵם כַּאֲשֶׁר גַּם־אָנֹכִי לֹא מִן־הָעוֹלָם אָנִי:

15 וְלֹא אַעְתִּיר לְךָ אֲשֶׁר תִּקָּחֵם מִן־הָעוֹלָם רַק שֶׁתִּצְּרֵם מִן־הָ רָע:

16 לֹא מִן־הָעוֹלָם הֵם כַּאֲשֶׁר גַּם־אָנֹכִי אֵינֶנִּי מִן־הָעוֹלָם:

17 קַדֵּשׁ אֹתָם בַּאֲמִתֶּךָ דְּבָרְךָ אֱמֶת:

18 כַּאֲשֶׁר אַתָּה שָׁלַחְתָּ אֹתִי אֶל־הָעוֹלָם כֵּן גַּם־אֲנִי שָׁלַחְתִּי אֹתָם אֶל־הָעוֹלָם:

19 וַאֲנִי מַקְדִּישׁ אֶת־נַפְשִׁי בַּעֲדָם לְמַעַן יִהְיוּ גַם־הֵם מְקֻדָּשִׁים בֶּאֱמֶת:

11 And now I am no more in the world, but these are in the world, and I come to thee. Holy Father, keep through thine own name those whom thou hast given me, that they may be one, as we are.

12 While I was with them in the world, I kept them in thy name: those that thou gavest me I have kept, and none of them is lost, but the son of Abaddon; that the scripture might be fulfilled.

13 And now come I to thee; and these things I speak in the world, that they might have my joy fulfilled in themselves.

14 I have given them thy word; and the world hath hated them, because they are not of the world, even as I am not of the world.

15 I pray not that thou shouldest take them out of the world, but that thou shouldest keep them from the Evil One.

16 They are not of the world, even as I am not of the world.

17 Sanctify them through thy truth: thy word is truth.

18 As thou hast sent me into the world, even so have I also sent them into the world.

19 And for their sakes I sanctify myself, that they also might be sanctified through the truth.

20 אוּלָם לֹא לְבַד בְּעַד־אֵלֶּה אָנֹכִי מַעְתִּיר לָךְ כִּי אִם־גַּם־בְּעַד הַמַּאֲמִינִים בִּי עַל־פִּי דְבָרָם:

21 לְמַעַן יִהְיוּ כֻלָּם אֶחָד כַּאֲשֶׁר אַתָּה אָבִי בִּי אַתָּה וַאֲנִי בָךְ וְהָיוּ גַם־הֵמָּה בָּנוּ כְּאֶחָד לְמַעַן יַאֲמִין הָעוֹלָם כִּי אַתָּה שְׁלַחְתָּנִי:

22 וַאֲנִי נָתַתִּי לָהֶם אֶת־הַכָּבוֹד אֲשֶׁר נָתַתָּ לִי לְמַעַן יִהְיוּ אֶחָד כַּאֲשֶׁר אֲנַחְנוּ אֶחָד:

23 אֲנִי בָהֶם וְאַתָּה בִּי לְמַעַן יִהְיוּ מֻשְׁלָמִים לְאֶחָד וּלְמַעַן יֵדַע הָעוֹלָם כִּי אַתָּה שְׁלַחְתָּנִי וְאָהַבְתָּ אֹתָם כַּאֲשֶׁר אֲהַבְתָּנִי:

24 אָבִי אֲשֶׁר נְתַתָּם לִי רְצוֹנִי שֶׁיִּהְיוּ עִמָּדִי בַּאֲשֶׁר אֶהְיֶה אָנִי לְמַעַן יֶחֱזוּ בִכְבוֹדִי אֲשֶׁר נָתַתָּ לִי כִּי אֲהַבְתָּנִי לִפְנֵי מוֹסְדוֹת עוֹלָם:

25 אָבִי הַצַּדִּיק הֵן הָעוֹלָם לֹא יְדָעֶךָ וַאֲנִי יְדַעְתִּיךָ וְאֵלֶּה הִכִּירוּ אֲשֶׁר אַתָּה שְׁלַחְתָּנִי:

26 וַאֲנִי הוֹדַעְתִּים אֶת־שִׁמְךָ וְאוֹסִיף לְהוֹדִיעָם לְמַעַן תִּהְיֶה־ בָּם הָאַהֲבָה אֲשֶׁר אֲהַבְתָּנִי וְגַם אֲנִי אֶהְיֶה בָהֶם:

20 Neither pray I for these alone, but for them also which shall believe on me through their word;

21 That they all may be one; as thou, Father, art in me, and I in thee, that they also may be one in us: that the world may believe that thou hast sent me.

22 And the glory which thou gavest me I have given them; that they may be one, even as we are one:

23 I in them, and thou in me, that they may be made perfect in one; and that the world may know that thou hast sent me, and hast loved them, as thou hast loved me.

24 Father, I will that they also, whom thou hast given me, be with me where I am; that they may behold my glory, which thou hast given me: for thou lovedst me before the foundation of the world.

25 O righteous Father, the world hath not known thee: but I have known thee, and these have known that thou hast sent me.

26 And I have declared unto them thy name, and will declare it: that the love wherewith thou hast loved me may be in them. and I in them.

Hebrew/English Index

	Hebrew	English	Strong	Verb Ster
1	אָב	Father	H1	Noun
2	אָבַד	Lost	H6	Pa, Pi, Hi
3	אָהַב	Love	H157	Paal, Piel
4	אָח	Brother	H251	Noun
5	אֶחָד	One	H259	Adjectice
6	אַף	Nose	H639	Noun
7	בּוֹא (בָּא)	Came	H935	Pa, Hi, Ho
8	בֶּגֶד	Clothes	H899	Noun
9	גָּג	Roof	H1406	Noun
10	גָּד	Troop	H1409	Noun
11	גּוּד	Overcame	H1464	Paal
12	דָּג	Fish	H1709	Noun
13	דּוֹד	Uncle	H1730	Noun
14	דּוּד	Pot	H1731	Noun
15	דָּוִד	David	H1732	Noun
16	דּוֹדָה	Aunt	H1733	Noun
17	הַבְהָב	Offering	H1890	Noun
18	הָגָה	Meditate	H1897	Paal

Hebrew/English Index

19	הוּא	He	H1931	Pronoun
20	הוֹד	Beauty	H1935	Paal
21	הוֹדָה	Confessed	(H3034)	Pa, Pi, Hi, Hit
22	הָיָה	(He) Was	H1961	Pa, Ni
23	וָו	Hook	H2053	Noun
24	זֶבֶד	Dowry	H2065	Noun
25	זֶה	This	H2088	Pronoun
26	זָהָב	Gold	H2091	Noun
27	זוּב	Overflowed	H2100	Pa
28	חַג	Feast	H2282	Noun
29	חָגָב	Locust	H2284	Noun
30	חוּג	Circle	H2328	Paal
31	חֹזֶה	Seer	H2374	Noun
32	חָטָא	Sin	H2398	Pa, Pi, Hi, Hit
33	טוֹב	Good	H2896	Paal
34	טָוָה	Spun	H2901	Paal
35	טָחָה	Archer	H2909	Piel
36	יָד	Hand	H3027	Noun
37	יְהוָה	Yᴀʜᴏᴡᴀʜ	H3068	Noun

Hebrew/English Index

38	יָחַד	United	H3161	Pa, Pi
39	יָחִיד	Only	H3173	Adjective
40	יָטַב	Succeeded	H3190	Pa, Hi
41	כּוֹבֶד	Heavy	H3514	Noun
42	כַּד	Pitcher	H3537	Noun
43	כֹּחַ	Strength	H3581	Noun
44	כּוֹהֵן	Priest	H3548	Noun
45	כּוֹכָב	Star	H3556	Noun
46	כֵּן	Yes	H3651	Adjective, Adverb
47	כֶּסֶף	Silver	H3701	Noun
48	לֹא	No	H3808	Adverb
49	לְבַד	Alone		
50	לָהַט	Burned	H3857	Pa, Pi
51	לוּחַ	Tablet	H3871	Noun
52	לֶחֶם	Bread	H3899	Noun
53	לָכַד	Captured	H3920	Pa, Ni, Hit
54	מִגְדָּל	Tower	H4026	Noun
55	מַיִם	Water	H4325	Noun
56	מִיץ	Juice	H4330	Noun
57	מַלְאָךְ	Angel	H4397	Noun

Hebrew/English Index

58	מִלְחָמָה	Fight	H4421	Noun
59	מֶלֶךְ	King	H4428	Noun
60	נָבִיא	Prophet	H5030	Noun
61	נָגִיד	Prince	H5057	Noun
62	נָטָה	Stretched	H5186	Pa, Ni, Hi
63	נָתַן	Gave	H5414	Pa, Ni, Ho
64	סָבִיב	Compass	H5439	Adjective, Adverb
65	סוּס	Horse	H5483	Noun
66	סֻכָּה	Booth	H5521	Noun
67	סָלַח	Forgave	H5545	Pa, Ni
68	סָמַךְ	Support	H5564	Pa, Ni, Pi
69	עָבַד	Worked	H5647	Pa, Ni, Pu, Hi, Ho
70	עוֹלָם	World	H5769	Noun
71	עָמַד	Stood	H5975	Pa, Hi, Ho
72	עָנָה	Answered	H6030	Pa, Ni
73	עֵץ	Tree	H6086	Noun
74	פָּגַע	Striked	H6293	Pa, Hi
75	פָּנִים	Face	H6440	Noun
76	פְּעֻלָּה	Payment	H6468	Noun
77	צְבִי	Deer	H6643	Noun

Hebrew/English Index

78	צוּד	Hunted	H6679	Pa, Po, Hi
79	צָחַק	Laughed	H6711	Pa, Pi
80	קָבַל	Received	H6901	Pi, Hi
81	קֶדֶם	Ancient	H6924	Noun
82	קָהַל	Assembly	H6950	Ni, Hi
83	קוּם	Rise	H6965	Pa, Pi, Hi, Ho, Hit,
84	רָאָה	See	H7200	Pa, Ni, Pu Hi, Ho, Hit
85	רֶגֶל	Leg	H7272	Noun
86	רוּחַ	Spirit	H7307	Noun
87	רָפָא (רוֹפֵא)	Doctor	H7495	Pa, Ni, Pi, Hit
88	רָצָה	Wanted	H7521	Pa, Ni, Pi, Hi, Hit
89	שִׁיר	Sing	H7892	Noun
90	שָׁכַב	Lay	H7901	Pa, Ni, Pu Hi, Ho
91	שָׁלוֹם	Peace	H7965	Noun
92	שָׂדֶה	Field	H7704	Noun
93	שׂוּם (שִׂים)	Put	H7760	Pa, Hi, Ho
94	שָׂמֵחַ	Rejoiced	H8056	Adjective
95	תּוֹדה	Thanks	H8426	Noun
96	תּוֹרה	Law	H8451	Noun

97	תְּמוּנָה	Picture	H8544	Noun
98	תִּקְוָה	Hope	H8615	Noun

	Hebrew	English	Strong	Verb Ste
English/Hebrew Index				
	Hebrew	**English**	**Strong**	**Verb Ste**
1	**Alone**	לְבַד		
2	**Ancient**	קֶדֶם	H6924	Noun
3	**Angel**	מַלְאָךְ	H4397	Noun
4	**Answered**	עָנָה	H6030	Pa, Ni
5	**Archer**	טָחָה	H2909	Piel
6	**Assembly**	קָהָל	H6950	Ni, Hi
7	**Aunt**	דּוֹדָה	H1733	Noun
8	**Beauty**	הוֹד	H1935	Paal
9	**Booth**	סֻכָּה	H5521	Noun
10	**Bread**	לֶחֶם	H3899	Noun
11	**Brother**	אָח	H251	Noun
12	**Burned**	לָהַט	H3857	Pa, Pi
13	**Came**	בּוֹא (בָּא)	H935	Pa, Hi, Ho
14	**Captured**	לָכַד	H3920	Pa, Ni, Hit
15	**Circle**	חוּג	H2328	Paal
16	**Clothes**	בֶּגֶד	H899	Noun
17	**Compass**	סָבִיב	H5439	Adjective, Adverb
18	**Confessed**	הוֹדָה	(H3034)	Pa, Pi, Hi, Hit

English/Hebrew Index

19	David	דָּוִד	H1732	Noun
20	Deer	צְבִי	H6643	Noun
21	Doctor	רָפָא (רוֹפֵא)	H7495	Pa, Ni, Pi, Hit
22	Dowry	זֶבֶד	H2065	Noun
23	Face	פָּנִים	H6440	Noun
24	Father	אָב	H1	Noun
25	Feast	חַג	H2282	Noun
26	Field	שָׂדֶה	H7704	Noun
27	Fight	מִלְחָמָה	H4421	Noun
28	Fish	דָּג	H1709	Noun
29	Forgave	סָלַח	H5545	Pa, Ni
30	Gave	נָתַן	H5414	Pa, Ni, Ho
31	Gold	זָהָב	H2091	Noun
32	Good	טוֹב	H2896	Paal
33	Hand	יָד	H3027	Noun
34	He	הוּא	H1931	Pronoun
35	Heavy	כּוֹבֶד	H3514	Noun
36	Hook	וָו	H2053	Noun
37	Hope	תִּקְוָה	H8615	Noun
38	Horse	סוּס	H5483	Noun

39	Hunted	צוּד	H6679	Pa, Po, Hi
40	Juice	מִיץ	H4330	Noun
41	King	מֶלֶךְ	H4428	Noun
42	Laughed	צָחַק	H6711	Pa, Pi
43	Law	תּוֹרָה	H8451	Noun
44	Lay	שָׁכַב	H7901	Pa, Ni, Pu Hi, Ho
45	Leg	רֶגֶל	H7272	Noun
46	Locust	חָגָב	H2284	Noun
47	Lost	אָבַד	H6	Pa, Pi, Hi
48	Love	אָהַב	H157	Pa, Pi
49	Meditate	הָגָה	H1897	Paal
50	No	לֹא	H3808	Adverb
51	Nose	אַף	H639	Noun
52	Offering	הַבְהָב	H1890	Noun
53	One	אֶחָד	H259	Adjectice
54	Only	יָחִיד	H3173	Adjective
55	Overcame	גּוּד	H1464	Paal
56	Overflowed	זוּב	H2100	Pa
57	Payment	פְּעֻלָּה	H6468	Noun
58	Peace	שָׁלוֹם	H7965	Noun

English/Hebrew Index

59	Picture	תְּמוּנָה	H8544	Noun
60	Pitcher	כַּד	H3537	Noun
61	Pot	דּוּד	H1731	Noun
62	Priest	כּוֹהֵן	H3548	Noun
63	Prince	נָגִיד	H5057	Noun
64	Prophet	נָבִיא	H5030	Noun
65	Put	שׂוֹם (שִׂים)	H7760	Pa, Hi, Ho
66	Received	קָבַל	H6901	Pi, Hi
67	Rejoiced	שָׂמֵחַ	H8056	Adjective
68	Rise	קוּם	H6965	Pa, Pi, Hi, Ho, Hit,
69	Roof	גָּג	H1406	Noun
70	See	רָאָה	H7200	Pa, Ni, Pu, Hi, Ho, Hit
71	Seer	חֹזֶה	H2374	Noun
72	Silver	כֶּסֶף	H3701	Noun
73	Sin	חָטָא	H2398	Pa, Pi, Hi, Hit
74	Sing	שִׁיר	H7892	Noun
75	Spirit	רוּחַ	H7307	Noun
76	Spun	טָוָה	H2901	Paal
77	Star	כּוֹכָב	H3556	Noun

78	Stood	עָמַד	H5975	Pa, Hi, Ho
79	Strength	כֹּחַ	H3581	Noun
80	Stretched	נָטָה	H5186	Pa, Ni, Hi
81	Striked	פָּגַע	H6293	Pa, Hi
82	Succeeded	יָטַב	H3190	Pa, Hi
83	Support	סָמַךְ	H5564	Pa, Ni, Pi
84	Tablet	לוּחַ	H3871	Noun
85	Thanks	תּוֹדָה	H8426	Noun
86	This	זֶה	H2088	Pronoun
87	Tower	מִגְדָּל	H4026	Noun
88	Tree	עֵץ	H6086	Noun
89	Troop	גָּד	H1409	Noun
90	Uncle	דּוֹד	H1730	Noun
91	United	יָחַד	H3161	Pa, Pi
92	Wanted	רָצָה	H7521	Pa, Ni, Pi, Hi, Hit
93	(He) Was	הָיָה	H1961	Pa, Ni
94	Water	מַיִם	H4325	Noun
95	Worked	עָבַד	H5647	Pa, Ni, Pu, Hi, Ho
96	World	עוֹלָם	H5769	Noun

English/Hebrew Index			
97	Yahowah	יְהֹוָה	H3068	Noun
98	Yes	כֵּן	H3651	Adjective, Adverb